An Agent Tells All

An Agent Tells All

Tony Martinez

HIT TEAM Publishing

An Agent Tells All

Copyright © 2005 by Tony Martinez

HIT TEAM Publishing
269 South Beverly Drive
#956
Beverly Hills, California 90212

Printed in the United States of America

Cover Design: Michael Cox
Printed by McNaughton & Gunn

First Edition

Library of Congress Control Number
2004112228

ISBN 0-9761433-0-5

Books may be purchased in bulk at special discounts for promotional and educational purposes. All inquiries should be addressed to Hit Team Publishing at the above address.

Table of Contents

Introduction

I don't represent Tom Cruise.

I've been a Hollywood agent for over ten years and in that time, I have always worked in the trenches, representing working actors and new performers who are just getting started.

Over the years, I've met thousands of actors and they always ask the same questions. Year after year. The questions never change. And that's why I wrote this book. It's my way of answering those questions.

There are plenty of books on the market written by people who have no business giving advice to actors. Half the time, I don't even know what they're talking about. I've always told my friends that someone like me, a working agent, could easily do better.

So the time has come to put up or shut up. My goal is to give you good, solid advice without pulling any punches. I also want to help you understand how agents think and how we really feel about actors.

I wrote this book for those of you who are just starting out in your career. I also wrote it for all the actors who have been struggling for years and just can't seem to catch a break.

I didn't write this book for Tom Cruise. He seems to be doing just fine.

Let's Talk About Agents

"An agent gives the actor a sense of stature and dignity... the agent believes in your work when you are certain you will never work again...the agent gives the actor access, opportunity and support."

— Colleen Dewhurst

Let's Talk About Agents 1

If you want to succeed as an actor, there's something you need to know. <u>Agents are absolutely necessary</u>. It's like knowing the guy at the door of a private club. We can get you inside.

Having an agent makes you acceptable to the entertainment industry. In a sense, when an agent signs you, they're acting as a filter for the casting community, screening out the untalented and deciding who is legitimate and worth knowing.

Agents also act as your defender, insuring that when you're offered employment, you will receive the best deal possible. They will make certain that no one is allowed to take advantage of you or your desire to work.

And when you have an agent, you get to say cool things like, "call my agent".

A Little Bit About Me

When I tell people what I do for a living, they always want to know why I became an agent. The answer is simple. I lost a bet. But I'll get to that in a minute.

Once upon a time, I graduated from film school in New York. If you want to see my degree, I'll be happy to dig it out of the closet and blow off the dust. No one in this business has ever expressed interest in my education. Surprised?

After graduating, I bounced around as a freelance cameraman. I was the guy you would hire to go anywhere and film anything.

Here are some of the more unusual jobs I performed:

1. I once spent a week in Birmingham, Alabama filming live surgery.
2. Another time, a famous psychic hired me to camp out in a New Jersey cemetery, so I could capture footage of a ghost that never showed.
3. And then there was the summer I worked in Central America, documenting illegal factory conditions.

(Quick piece of advice: If you're ever stopped by border patrol guards, don't mouth off! Spending the night in a Haitian jail isn't nearly as much fun as you would think.)

Returning to New York, I ended up part of the local production scene. I started off as a location scout, hustled my way up to production manager and eventually became a music video producer.

Over the years, I helped produce over thirty videos for artists like The Beastie Boys, Run-DMC and The Black Crowes.

Then, as I was about to turn 30, I decided it was time for a change. The whole production scene had become boring. And I didn't want to live in New York for the rest of my life.

So I packed my bags and headed west.

When I arrived in LA, I had a lot of money and no job. Six months later, I had spent the money and still had no job.

So one night, I was hanging out in a Hollywood bar called "The Cat and the Fiddle" with an actor friend named Mike. He was keeping me company while I searched through the want ads in the back of *Variety*.

We noticed one that said:

AGENT'S ASSISTANT
Major Talent Agency Seeks Assistant
Long Hours/Low Pay

Mike thought it was perfect for me. He explained that agents rule the business and working at an agency would be a great way to learn more about LA.

I wasn't so sure. For starters, I used to have my own assistant back in New York. This felt like a step backwards. I was also more than a little concerned about the whole "long hours/low pay" thing.

We argued back and forth like two drunken idiots, and then we decided to flip a coin. As luck would have it, I lost the toss.

So the next day, I sent in my resume and three interviews later, I was hired as an assistant at Paradigm, one of the largest talent agencies in LA. Their client list included actors like Andy Garcia, Kenneth Branagh and Laurence Fishburne.

After going through their training program for almost two years, I moved to a smaller agency and became a licensed, fully franchised, Hollywood talent agent.

And that's what I've been doing for the last ten years.

All because I lost a bet.

The Life of an Agent

So what exactly is an agent? I'll make it simple. Agents are middlemen, brokering the talent of others in return for ten percent of their income. In other words, we're glorified salesmen. Instead of selling real estate or used cars, we sell actors.

But as usual, there's much more to it than that. People are always asking me to explain what I do. Sure, being an agent sounds glamorous, but just what the hell do we do all day?

It's a tough question to answer but the way I see it, my entire job can be broken down into three basic elements:

1: SIGNING
2: SERVICING
3: SELLING

Okay, let's take it one at a time. In my opinion, the most important one is...

Signing

There's a dirty little secret that agents don't want you to know. We need you as much as you need us.

Think about it. If all the agents in LA were to suddenly vanish, actors would go right on working. Managers and lawyers would step up, negotiate the deals and life would go on.

But what if all the actors disappeared? I'd be out of a job or at the very least, I would have to find someone else to represent. Maybe writers. Are they any saner than actors?

One thing to keep in mind is that an agent's status is measured by the quality of his client list. This is why we're always on the prowl for new talent. It's how we make our living.

A few years ago, a friend dragged me to see a play at some hole in the wall theater in downtown LA. It was a terrible neighborhood and I really didn't want to go.

Sure enough, the play was awful but there was a young actor on stage who was absolutely terrific. Without a doubt, he was the best thing in the show.

I brought him in for a meeting and we ended up signing him on the spot. At the time, his resume wasn't much more than a blank piece of paper but you know what? Within six months, he booked a series regular role on a hit NBC show. This guy went from barely surviving to making almost $250,000 in his first year as a professional actor.

Do you see why signing is the most important part of my job?

There's nothing more validating to an agent than discovering someone who is brand new to the business and getting them started on the road to a successful acting career.

Naturally, we also spend a great deal of time trying to sign established talent. In other words, we're always looking to steal actors from other agencies. This is part of the job and I have no moral problems doing it. After all, you can't steal a client who doesn't want to be stolen.

Case in point. I once ran into a rival agent at a Friday night screening. She announced that she had just quit her job and was moving back to Chicago. The owners had gotten the news from her a few hours earlier, just as they were closing for the weekend.

And that's when the light bulb went on over my head. I realized there hadn't been enough time to inform their clients!

There happened to be an actor at that company who I was extremely interested in signing. I had been pursuing him for several months and luckily, I had his number in my cell phone's memory.

So what did I do? I called him from the screening and asked how he felt about his agent quitting the business. The guy was stunned. This was news to him. He was also furious that he was hearing it from me, and not from one of his own agents.

That's all it took. The dominoes started falling and by the end of the following week, the actor jumped ship and signed with my agency.

So the thing to remember here is that we're always looking for new clients — experienced and new. Have you ever had an agent tell you "sorry, we're not looking right now"?

Well, just as you suspected, they're lying. What they really mean is, we're not looking for you right now. It's just a nicer way of saying the same thing.

Don't forget — Hollywood is a town where the greeting "hello" is considered a lie.

Servicing

Now, once I sign an actor, that person becomes my responsibility. I don't just put their name on a list and forget about them. That's a recipe for disaster. An agent has to take care of his clients.

I go through my list every month and check to see who hasn't been going out on auditions. Then I give those actors a call, just to touch base and reassure them that they haven't been forgotten.

I also keep an eye on clients who are auditioning but not booking work. They may need extra attention and possibly advice on finding a good coach.

Servicing also means visiting actors on set, showing up at their parties, helping with personal problems, and a million other little things.

Unfortunately, it's impossible to give every single client the same amount of attention. There just aren't enough hours in the day. So an agent has to prioritize. And quite often, that decision is based on money.

Here's a statistic every agent knows:

Ten percent of your client list generates ninety percent of your income.

Keeping that in mind, you can bet your bottom dollar that those top clients are going to get plenty of attention. Their calls will always get through. They will never feel like they've been forgotten.

A large part of my day is spent making sure that I keep those important clients happy, especially during the slow periods. Because if I don't, some other agent might steal them away. And that's not acceptable.

Now that doesn't mean I ignore the other ninety percent. It's my goal to give everyone a realistic amount of time and attention. This is crucial because you never know who's going to hit.

I once represented an actress named Becky who starred on a famous sitcom back in the eighties. Unfortunately, that damn show typecast her for life. Everybody knew Becky but no one would hire her. As a result, she hadn't worked in several years.

I was getting ready to drop her when all of a sudden, she got an audition for the lead in a new TV series. The creators had been big fans when they were growing up and now they wanted to meet her.

As luck would have it, Becky booked the job. She ended up working on the show for three years and made over a million dollars!

Luckily, I had treated her well during those lean years and she never forgot that. So when a bigger agency tried to steal her, Becky stayed put. In this case, servicing a low priority client paid off in a big way.

And she never found out how close she came to getting the axe.

Selling

Show business has always been made up of two very distinct groups of people — buyers and sellers. Here's how it breaks down:

Buyer	Seller	The Product
Casting Director	Me	You

Simple but true. Here's another way of looking at the same concept:

> Actors need...
> Agents, who sell to...
> Casting Directors, who work for...
> Producers and Directors, who answer to...
> Studios and Networks.

That's the Hollywood food chain. Did you notice how far down actors are on the list? Don't feel bad. Agents aren't much higher.

(Please note that we're not talking about movie stars here. Actors like Mel Gibson and Julia Roberts are part of a completely different food chain.)

Selling is a very important part of an agent's job because bookings are what keep an agency in business. Without commissions, a good company can end up having to close their doors.

That's why it doesn't matter if a client is established or brand new. Agents will push the actor they feel has the greatest chance of booking a role.

We know that even a relative newcomer can book a series regular role on a new TV show and start making $20,000 an episode.

Let's take a moment and do the math.

A half-hour sitcom takes 5 days to shoot and a one-hour drama usually takes 8. That's $20,000 for less than 2 weeks work. Pretty impressive, right?

But wait! The numbers get better. Consider that most shows shoot 22 episodes in a year and that a production year is only 8 months long.

$$\begin{array}{r} \$20,000 \text{ per show} \\ \underline{\times\ 22 \text{ shows}} \\ \$440,000 \end{array}$$

So we're talking close to half a million dollars a year with a four-month break between seasons. Not bad, huh?

There's a lot of dumb money in Hollywood and everybody wants some.

That's why a big part of my job is making sure that clients get a chance to audition for every role that's right for them. This is much easier said than done.

One of the tools that agents use to keep track of projects is called *The Breakdowns*.

Every day, a company called "Breakdown Services" delivers a thick stack of casting notices to every agency in town. These breakdowns list the casting needs of all the film and TV shows that are currently in production.

Here's an example of a role that was recently available on a big movie:

[NICK] Caucasian, age 18 to 21, good looking and athletic. Nick is innately intelligent and thoughtful, with a philosophical bent, and is the moral compass in his family. LEAD

Agents spend most of their mornings pouring over these roles and submitting their best ideas for each one. Depending on the number of breakdowns, this process can easily take a couple of hours.

Picture it. Every agent in town, hunched over their desk, pen in hand, trying to figure out who can play a dead body on "Six Feet Under". What a weird way to make a living.

Anyway, our finished submissions, which are basically envelopes stuffed with pictures and resumes, are then messengered to the appropriate casting directors for their consideration.

These submissions can number in the hundreds. I once visited a casting director's office and saw all the envelopes they had received that day. The pile was over five feet tall!

As you can imagine, my job would be much easier if I didn't have so much competition. Unfortunately, there are over 100 licensed talent agencies in LA. I'm talking about huge companies like CAA down to tiny one-man shops where the agent answers his own phone.

For the record, the largest and most powerful agencies are:

> Creative Artists Agency (CAA)
> The William Morris Agency
> International Creative Management (ICM)
> The Gersh Agency
> United Talent Agency (UTA)
> Endeavor
> Paradigm
> Innovative

If you were to throw a stick down the hall at one of these places, you'd probably hit at least 2 or 3 celebrities.

Besides representing major stars, these companies also handle producers, directors, writers and other production personnel. Not much happens in this town without these people having a hand in it.

In addition to the big boys, there are over a hundred other agencies, each with anywhere from 100 to 500 clients.

Think about that for a moment. We're talking about hundreds of agents trying to secure work for thousands of clients on a daily basis.

This is why agents are always working the phones, trying to get casting directors to meet their clients. The calls never stop. There are only so many roles to go around and we're constantly pitching ideas for all of them.

Let's say that the casting director of "C.S.I." is looking for an attractive blonde to play a nurse in her early twenties. I would guess there are probably hundreds of women in LA who could easily play that part. The question is, how many will actually get a chance to read? Probably about ten.

And all ten of them will have an agent.

That's why it's crucial for agents to have excellent relationships with the casting community. It's important that our submissions get opened and that our phone calls get taken.

Agents work hard to earn the trust and respect of casting directors. And we do it by signing clients who will make us look good when we send them in to audition.

So again, it's all about signing. See how that came full circle?

The Agent/Client Relationship

Clients tend to be insecure about their relationship with their agents. Why? Because agents have more than one client. And actors always fear that another client will have a greater claim on our time.

This is why agents are rarely free to spend their entire day doing their job. We're too busy taking calls from worried clients.

When an actor calls over and over, asking why they haven't had any auditions, I usually tell them the same thing. "I don't have time to pitch you because I'm always stuck on the phone talking to you."

This usually stops the calls. But only for a while.

Academy Award winning director James Cameron once said, "The way the human immune system works is that there are antibodies which key into any organism that comes into the body. They will shape themselves to that organism. I think of directing as being an antibody; I have to reshape myself for every person on the set."

Agents work the same way. We deal with over a hundred neurotic personalities on a regular basis. So to have an effective relationship with all my clients, I have to figure out what each one wants me to be.

That leads to a lot of role playing. Here are some of the hats I've worn — a strict father figure, an understanding best friend, a marriage counselor, a drinking buddy, a social escort, and many more.

It's all about keeping everyone happy.

One of the hardest parts of my job is dealing with a client's failure. It's painful for everyone. There's a lot of personal hurt involved.

This is especially tricky because clients tend to handle failure by firing their agent. Why not respond to rejection by blaming it on someone else rather than your own shortcomings? Killing the messenger may not change anything but it sure makes you feel better.

Here's a great example of this. Patrick is a character actor in his forties with a pretty impressive resume. You would never know his name but if you saw Patrick's face, you would recognize him immediately. Hollywood will always belong to the young and beautiful but guys like Patrick are the bread and butter of the agency business.

Anyway, just like many athletes, Patrick once found himself in a major slump. I was getting him out on plenty of auditions but he just couldn't book. The feedback was always great. Everyone still loved him. But it just wasn't happening.

This slump went on for almost six months. I watched Patrick get more and more frustrated. As an agent, I knew the worm would turn but there was no convincing him of that. Patrick couldn't see the light at the end of the tunnel.

So he fired me. Patrick moved to another agency and booked on his very first audition — a supporting role in a major studio movie!

Does this mean that I wasn't doing my job? Of course not. Does this mean Patrick was right to leave? Well, yes and no.

Yes because on a mental level, maybe this change was just what he needed to shake himself out of the slump. And no, because I had been doing a great job, getting him out there, sticking with him during the bad times, and I should have been the one to profit when he finally scored.

And that's show business, folks.

Final Thoughts

I was once part of a panel discussion with several other agents about the business of acting. During a break, the guy next to me leaned over and said, "This would be a great job if it weren't for all the damn actors".

I promised myself that if I ever got that cynical, I would quit and open a tiki bar in the South Seas.

But on another level, I understood exactly what he was talking about. Agents often feel that actors go out of their way to make their life miserable. This is a shame because it really doesn't have to be that way.

After reading this book, I hope you'll have enough knowledge and information to avoid falling into that trap.

I also hope that when you're done reading, you'll know that I have absolutely nothing in common with the agent who made that joke.

Welcome to LA

"I'd move to Los Angeles if New Zealand and Australia were swallowed by a tidal wave, if there was a bubonic plague in England and if the continent of Africa disappeared from some Martian attack."

— Russell Crowe

Welcome to LA

There's no doubt about it. If you want to succeed as an actor, you have to move to LA. Why? Because that's where the action is, baby.

LA is the big time.

Sure, there's some film and TV work in New York but look at the numbers. At the moment, there are only 12 shows shooting in the Big Apple. Guess how many there are in LA? I stopped counting at 100.

And yes, there's plenty of stage work in New York. For that matter, there are terrific theaters all over this great nation. But who's kidding who? I have never met one single actor who didn't want to see his face on a forty-foot screen. Or at the very least, a 29-inch Sony.

So if you want to make a decent living and reach a large audience, you have to pack your bags and make the move to LA. It's the only real way to have a long-term career as an actor.

"I'm thinking about visiting for a few months so I can test the water. Is that a good idea?"

No, it's not. You can't expect anything major to happen in such a short period of time. It takes much longer to figure out if you really have a future in this business.

Most actors spend their first year in LA getting used to the city and trying to learn how the business works. Finding an agent and meeting all the right casting directors takes even longer.

If you're serious about your career, you have to commit to this town for at least three years. That should give you enough time to figure out if you're on the right track.

And if you're not, don't start thinking of yourself as a failure. This life isn't for everyone. I know a lot of great actors who never made it but went on to become very successful in other parts of the business.

"Okay. I've decided to move to Los Angeles. How do I get an agent?"

You don't. Getting an agent should be the last thing on your mind. Trust me. You're not ready.

The competition in LA is fierce. There are about 6 billion people on this planet and 2 billion are actors trying to make it in LA.

So before you jump in, you must be 100% prepared. It's crucial to get off to a good start because if you screw up the beginning, you'll never make it to the end.

So here are nine steps that will make your life a whole lot easier. It should take you about six months to work your way through the entire list. After that, you'll be ready to start looking for your first agent.

And don't skip this section if you already live here. You might find some useful information that you've overlooked.

Step One:
GET A JOB

Actors always make the move to LA with a hope and a prayer. They'd be better off bringing money.

This isn't a cheap town. Besides living expenses, you're going to need headshots, classes and a million other things. It's scary how this stuff can add up.

Getting a job should be a priority. It has to be one with flexible hours that will allow you time to audition. This can often be tricky. As a result, most new actors end up working more than one job.

Actors often make the mistake of thinking that waiter and bartender jobs are easy to find in LA. Not true. The good ones are already taken by actors who know a good thing when they see it. If your timing's good, you might luck into an opening but don't just assume it's going to be easy.

Another option is doing temp work. If you want to go this route, enroll immediately at all the major temp agencies, especially Friedman and All-Star. They will assign you short-term work at studios, networks and even talent agencies.

If you have the right personality, temping could be a great way to make connections. And since you're going to be working at many different locations, temping will also help you learn your way around town.

It's hard to pursue an acting career if you're constantly worrying about how you're going to feed yourself. So address your financial needs as quickly as possible. Trust me — you'll be much happier in the long run.

Step Two:
LEARN THE CITY

New actors drool at the idea of auditioning at real movie studios but most of them don't even know where Warner Brothers is located.

It's very important that you learn how to get around. And let me warn you right now. LA is a tricky town. It takes a while to get the hang of it.

This is especially hard for New Yorkers who are used to streets being numbered. It doesn't work that way here. Hell, I still get lost on San Vicente Boulevard and I've been living in LA for over ten years.

So get a map. Some people swear by the Thomas Brothers Guide. I've always found it bulky and difficult to read. The laminated Rand McNally is my favorite. It's up to you. Whatever works best.

The key to understanding this town is learning which way is north and west. Just remember, the hills are always north and the ocean is always west. Those are the only two directions that really matter. If you drive south for a few hours, you'll end up in Mexico. And I have no idea where east goes. It's never come up.

A quick glance at the grid and you should be able to spot all the major streets. Learn which ones run north and south (Cahuenga, Fairfax, Sepulveda), and which ones go east and west (Sunset, Melrose, Wilshire). Don't worry about how to pronounce these names. This takes years. Sometimes a lifetime.

Now locate all the major studios on your brand new map and plot directions on how to get there from your home. You should also pick out some famous landmarks and do the same thing.

The next move is to get out there and drive. Go everywhere. Get used to the idea of living in your car. You're going to be spending a lot of time behind the wheel.

And don't be afraid to get lost. When I first moved here, I would go out of my way to get lost. This would force me to learn the city quickly and as a result, I had some pretty cool adventures.

The key is to always remember what George Burns said when someone asked him if he had any advice for new actors:

"Stay on Fountain, as long as possible "

(If you live in LA, this joke makes perfect sense. If you just got here, you probably don't get it. But trust me. You will.)

Step Three:
CREATE A SUPPORT SYSTEM

People will tell you that LA is a lonely town. Well, they're right. When I moved out from New York, I was stunned at how hard it is to make friends.

Part of the problem is that LA isn't really a city. It's more like a sprawling suburb that seems to go on for ever and ever.

As a result, you end up living in your car and it's hard to meet people when you're stuck behind the wheel.

But no man is an island. You're going to need friends. So consider joining a theater company or an improv group. Besides meeting plenty of people, you'll also get to know other actors who can provide you with valuable information.

LA is an industry town. So accept the fact that most of your new friends are going to be in the business. And even if they're not, I guarantee they've written a screenplay and would love to show it to you.

Step Four:
READ THE TRADES

Everyone in the business reads "The Hollywood Reporter" and "Variety". These daily publications are the lifeline of the industry. Reading them will make you feel like you're in the game.

Unfortunately, these magazines ain't cheap. To save money, I suggest that you subscribe to just one of them. Or better still, get some actor friends to chip in and help offset the cost.

You should also buy a subscription to "Back Stage West". This weekly paper is geared towards struggling actors. It's full of valuable information, audition notices, and part-time job opportunities.

Every little bit of knowledge helps when you're trying to get a new business off the ground. Acting is no different. Studying and understanding the industry is a big part of your job.

Step Five:
GATHER YOUR TOOLS

When I use the word "tools", I'm talking about headshots, resumes and demo reels. These items are your calling card to the entertainment industry. Without them, you're dead in the water.

The next chapter is all about getting your tools together before you approach an agent. Stay tuned.

Step Six:
GET A COMMERCIAL AGENT

Why not? Even if you hate the idea of acting in commercials, money is money. The rent needs to be paid. And it's much easier to find a commercial agent than it is to get a theatrical one.

So as soon as your headshots are ready, send one to every commercial agency in town. If you have the right look, you'll probably get called in for a few meetings.

Improv training can also be helpful when you're looking for a commercial agent. Spontaneity is a big part of the audition process and if you can improvise, you stand a much greater chance of booking work.

You should also sign up for a Commercial Cold Reading Class or On Camera Workshop that has an agent night at the end. This means the teacher will invite commercial agents to scout the students during the final class.

I know plenty of actors making a really nice living doing commercials while they pursue more serious work.

It sure beats being a waiter.

Step Seven:
VOLUNTEER TO BE A READER

Casting directors are sometimes forced to read with actors because their assistants are stuck answering the phones. Don't you think they would welcome some free help?

So volunteer to be a reader. Write to every casting director in town and let them know you're available. Make it clear that you're not planning to bother anyone for an audition. All you want is a shot at a great learning experience.

If you write enough letters, someone will eventually accept your offer. Then it's up to you.

Once you're in the casting director's office, keep your mouth shut. You're there to lend a hand and that's it. If you try to push yourself on anyone, I guarantee you will not be invited back. Ever.

Working as a reader will give you a chance to listen in on every decision. You'll also learn first hand what works in an audition and what doesn't. Then when you finally get an agent, you'll be 100% ready to audition at any casting office in town.

Step Eight:
INTERN AT A TALENT AGENCY

Casting directors aren't the only ones who could use a little extra help. So if you can spare a few hours a week, you should consider interning at a talent agency.

This is fantastic idea because you'll get to experience first hand the inner workings of an agency. And let me tell you something. You just can't buy that kind of education.

At first, you'll probably be asked to help with filing and other simple duties. The agents probably won't pay much attention but if you continue to show up on a regular basis, people will begin to take notice. And if you play your cards right, you can make some great contacts for the future.

Speaking from experience, there are plenty of former interns out there who still call me for advice.

The trick is to never, ever cross the invisible line. It's okay to ask questions but the moment you approach an agent about representation, your ass will be out the door.

Step Nine:
HAVE SOME FUN!

Don't get so caught up in your acting career that you forget to have a good time. If you're going to survive this insane business, you need to enjoy your life.

LA has a great deal to offer. Take advantage of that. Check out the museums. Explore the canyons. And when you have time, take a drive out to the Mojave Desert. You'll be amazed at what you find.

Remember, this is the kind of town where you can go surfing and snow boarding — all on the same weekend. How's that for a wide range of possibilities?

So get out there and make the city your own. LA is now home. And in a couple of years, it might even start to feel like it.

Final Thoughts

As soon as actors arrive in LA, they start running around like mice in a maze, desperately trying to find an agent.

"Where are they?" "The agents must be here somewhere!" "Have you seen any?"

Slow down! There's no rush. We're not going anywhere. And besides, thanks to this chapter, you've got enough to keep you busy for at least six months.

Let's recap:

1) GET A JOB

2) LEARN THE CITY

3) CREATE A SUPPORT SYSTEM

4) READ THE TRADES

5) GATHER YOUR TOOLS

6) GET A COMMERCIAL AGENT

7) VOLUNTEER TO BE A READER

8) INTERN AT A TALENT AGENCY

9) HAVE SOME FUN!

Now that we're done, take a moment and look back at number 5. This is the one you absolutely must complete before you can even think about approaching someone like me.

That's why I devoted the entire next chapter to it.

Tools
of
the
Trade

"In Europe, an actor is an artist. In Hollywood, if he isn't working, he's a bum."

— Anthony Quinn

Tools of the Trade 3

There are some basic tools that you absolutely must have before you can expect an agent to consider taking you on as a client. When asked, most agents will list the following three items as being essential:

1) Headshot
2) Resume
3) Demo Reel

I believe there's a fourth one that is constantly overlooked. That is:

4) Training

Makes sense, right? We're usually so caught up in the business of acting that we forget about craft. And what could possibly be more important? The best headshot in the world won't help if you can't deliver the goods in a casting office. That said, let's rearrange the order:

1) Training
2) Headshot
3) Resume
4) Demo Reel

Take a close look at that list. While the four basic categories will always remain the same, the contents are going to be constantly evolving during your career. With or without an agent, these basic tools should always be undergoing change and growth.

Let's take a closer look at each of them.

Training

Acting is one of the few careers in this world that constantly attracts people with no training. I'm always meeting young actors who haven't done any real studying and yet, they still think they're ready to work. Can you imagine if doctors behaved this way?

Granted, there are plenty of people out there who possess natural acting ability but trust me, that will only get you so far. Craft and technique are still very important and that's why you absolutely, positively must always be in class.

"What acting class do you recommend?"

Different agents like different teachers. Want to know my favorites? Sorry. You've got the wrong guy. I don't have any favorites. YOU are the only one who can make that decision.

When asked about who I would recommend, I never name one particular person or school. If pressed, I'll usually list about five teachers but the ultimate choice is up to you.

Don't be lazy. No one can tell you where to study. You're going to have to go out there and do some homework. It's your responsibility to audit several classes, interview the students, and get as much information as humanly possible. This is one of those rare times when you are in control. Enjoy it.

Granted, there are several instructors in LA who are well known and respected among the agent community. Teachers like Larry Moss, Ivana Chubbuck and Brian Reise are incredibly talented instructors with impressive backgrounds and a variety of great classes. But for every one of these people, there are many others out there who are less known but equally good.

It all comes down to who's best for you. Some actors need kid gloves and respond well in a gentle, nurturing environment. Others prefer a tougher approach. These actors come to life in a more aggressive setting where they are constantly being pushed to their limits. Where would you be more comfortable?

What about size? How many students are in the class? How often will you get to work? That's important too. Some of the more popular schools are so crammed with students that you only get to put up work once in a blue moon. Sure, the school will look great on your resume but will you really get anything out of it?

And never, ever spend more than you can afford. It's not worth going into debt just so you can brag about studying with Mr. Pretentious at the Super Popular School of Acting. Paying more in no way guarantees a better class of education.

What about technique? Which is better — Meisner or Method? I don't know. What are you asking me for? Any agent who claims to favor one particular technique over another is full of you know what. Most agents aren't qualified to make that judgment and they certainly couldn't tell the difference in an actor's performance.

"Do agents prefer actors who have a theater degree?"

A lot of young actors think it's important to get a degree from a famous university like Yale or Julliard before they start to purse a career in acting. To be honest, I can't imagine a bigger waste of time.

The problem is that most college professors have no understanding of the entertainment industry. As a result, they end up weighing students down with rigid techniques that have no place in the real world.

I also feel these teachers are very good at destroying the spark that made you talented in the first place. I know several working actors who studied at famous schools and they've told me it took them years to unlearn all the bad habits they picked up in college.

Now, don't get me wrong. I have nothing against theater degrees. If you have one, that's just dandy. But I really think you're better off majoring in an unrelated field so that at least you'll have something to fall back on if your acting career doesn't work out.

"What impresses you about an actor's training?"

For me, it's variety. Let me explain what I mean. Remember Bruce Lee? He's still considered one of the greatest martial artists who ever lived. Do you know how he attained that level of ability? Bruce spent his entire life studying every martial art in the world. His background was in Chinese kung fu but he also trained in Japanese karate, American boxing, and many, many others. He took what he liked from each style, discarded the rest and created Jeet Kune Do, his own personal martial art.

I challenge you to do the same thing. As an actor, it is your duty to get out there and learn as much as possible about the craft of acting. Try everything at least once. See what works for you. You will end up bringing a little bit of each technique to your own personal style.

Amy is one of my younger clients and she recently took a break from her scene study class and signed up for a summer program in Shakespeare. Surprised, I asked why she had done this.

"My friends aren't really into Shakespeare but I kind of like it. So I thought it would be fun to see if I could do it. Are you upset?"

Upset? Amy is now one of my favorite clients. She may never need to audition in iambic pentameter but after this program, not only will she be a better actress, Amy will be a more "fearless" actress. And that's money in the bank for me!

When I'm looking at a resume, I also like to see commitment. I want to know that you're dedicated to your career and working hard at your craft.

I recently took a meeting with an actress who moved out from New York and had been living here for over a year. Her resume had plenty of New York training on it but I didn't see any LA teachers. When I asked her about this, she told me that she hadn't gotten around to it yet.

Excuse me? How can someone live in LA for that long, surrounded by actors, and not act? It doesn't make any sense. If you love acting, you have to act. It's that simple.

Needless to say, I passed.

"Okay, that's what you like about training. What don't you like?"

Three words — the guru mentality. I often look at an actor's resume and see that he has studied with the same teacher for a very long time. This means he has turned that teacher into a guru and the class has now become a safe place. There is no way he's still being challenged in such a familiar environment. Where's the risk?

> "Art is unthinkable without risk."
> -Louis Pasternack

The business of acting is a pretty scary thing. Success is often based on luck and timing, not skill and ability. It's one of the few jobs out there where talent doesn't guarantee that you will work.

So actors seek out safety and comfort. They think that worshipping the same teacher for years will somehow give them a leg up in the business.

Wrong! You should never get trapped in the guru mentality. It leads to laziness and you will end up being a limited actor. Never, ever study with the same teacher for more than two years. Please trust me on this. Everyone's afraid of change but change is the most natural thing in the world. It's growing stagnant that's scary, especially if you're an artist.

So move on! Face some new challenges. Sick of scene study? Fine. Take a movement class. Tired of learning lines? Okay. Try an improv class. But keep growing and evolving as an actor. Training is the one thing that you should never stop. There's no end to it. And if you don't agree with me, then you won't be represented by me.

Don't forget, a large part of my ability to sell you as an actor will depend on how good you are at acting.

Headshots

Headshots are black and white, eight by ten inch photographs that strike fear and terror in the hearts of every single actor on the face of this planet.

Why? Because your headshot is your number one calling card, an extremely important marketing tool that has to capture your very soul in the click of a shutter. The right headshot can create endless opportunities; the wrong one can be the first nail in your career's coffin.

Every agent has the same complaint. We get a headshot in the mail and when we call in the actor, he looks nothing like his picture. You would be shocked at how many times this happens. And let me tell you something, meetings that start off on a bad note usually go nowhere fast.

The first rule of headshots is that the damn thing should look like you. Why try to create a false impression? Do you really want to see a look of disappointment when you walk into an agent's office?

So please don't try to hide your age, weight, lack of hair, scars or anything else that makes you feel insecure. Your headshot is not a personal ad. You need to be honest.

"What other mistakes do actors make?"

I once met with a talented young man named Scott who had a very preppy, collegiate look. Besides some impressive theater credits, he didn't have much work experience.

When Scott handed me his headshot, I thought I was looking at the wrong guy. His hair was greasy, his face unshaven, and he was a wearing an old leather jacket.

Now, as an actor, Scott has the right to play any role he wants. The best actors can transcend type. But Scott is just starting out. This isn't the time to worry about type casting. And quite frankly, there wasn't anything remotely dangerous about him.

I tried to explain my views but he just wouldn't listen. So I passed. Life is too short.

When actors try to create a false impression, it just tips me off that they're not in touch with themselves. They have no sense of how they fit into the marketplace. And this usually scares me off. I quickly realize that I'll never be able to represent them well because we have such different views of how they should be cast.

Here are some more basic don'ts about headshots:

DON'T wear a costume. Pictures of you in a lab coat or police uniform should be submitted to a commercial agency. They have no place in a theatrical agency. And they look silly.

DON'T use props. I've seen pictures of actors holding guns, tennis racquets, pets and I once saw a shot of a guy eating pasta. We all laughed at that one. Then we threw it out. Just say no to props.

DON'T take action shots. I hate pictures of actors running, dancing or working out. The only exception is if you're a martial artist. Those pictures sometimes come in handy. But I would consider it a specialized shot, not your main one.

"So describe the perfect headshot."

That's a hard question. I usually know it when I see it but it's very difficult to put into words. Let's try breaking it down into individual elements.

The first thing I notice is the subject's eyes. They have to be alive. I need to see something there. Avoid shots where your eyes are at half-mast. Look for the spark. Find the life. I know that sounds vague but you'll know what I'm talking about when you see it.

You should also avoid shots where the camera is in really tight on your face. I find these overwhelming and they tend to hide your personality. Give the picture a little room to breathe. By the same token, I don't care for full body shots. They tend to distance the subject from the camera. And that doesn't work either.

If you're an attractive woman, it's fine to go with a sexy shot but please remember that there's a fine line between sexy and slutty. I often see pictures of women in lingerie and other revealing outfits. I've even seen one where the actress is topless and covering her breasts with her hands.

As a man, I enjoy these shots a great deal and usually pass them around the office. But as an agent, I have no use for them. They're too extreme. I'm looking for a total package, not just body parts.

And do me a favor. Please make sure your headshot is in focus. Is that asking too much? I'm stunned at how many times I come across pictures that are soft. How hard is it to focus a damn camera? Maybe some actors think that a soft shot will make them look younger. It won't. It will just make you look fuzzy.

Keep in mind that it's hard to be objective about yourself — especially when you're looking at pictures. I would suggest that you show your proofs to people who know you really well. See what they think. If everyone agrees on the same shot, then you're good to go.

"What about clothes?"

You should definitely give careful consideration to what you wear. The picture needs to capture your personality. Try to pick clothes that make you feel comfortable. Avoid the fancy outfits and busy patterns that draw attention to themselves. The picture is supposed to be about you, not your clothes.

Keep in mind that black and white photography is all about shades of gray. So before you pick your clothes, empower yourself by reading up on how different colors photograph in black and white. This knowledge will help you make the right decision.

For example, you should never wear black. Black has no detail. You're better off going with red. White is also a bad idea. It tends to wash out. Try light gray instead.

As I write this book, there's a new trend towards color headshots. Thanks to digital photography, it's much more affordable now than when I first started as an agent. Frankly, I think it's only a matter of time before black and white is completely phased out.

So should you get color pictures? It's up to you. Redheads definitely benefit, as do actors with dark skin. I have a client from India and black and white has never done her justice. But color? Forget about it. She looks incredible.

"How many headshots do I need?"

When all is said and done, I usually end up working with two pictures. The variations depend on the individual. Dramatic and light, upscale and casual, whatever. Just limit it to two. Any more is overkill. It also creates storage problems for my assistant.

And finally, please have your name printed at the bottom of your pictures. Resumes often get separated from headshots and you don't want to be a nameless face on an agent's desk.

"How do I find the right photographer?"

The fairy tales were right. You have to kiss a lot of frogs before you find a prince.

If you've been following my advice, you should be in a good acting class by now. So talk to the other students and ask to see their headshots. Do the pictures look like them? Did the photographer capture their personality?

You should also find out if your friends enjoyed the shoot. Was the studio comfortable? Did they have a good time? Would they go back and use the same photographer again? These are all very important questions.

Remember, no one finds a good photographer through an ad in the trades. Word of mouth rules in this business.

Now you need to ask yourself if you would prefer a man or a woman. That's an important issue and often gets overlooked. So give it serious thought. Some people have trouble being themselves if they're around the opposite sex. And what if your goal is to express sexuality in your headshot? Which gender will make you comfortable enough to do that?

Once your research is done, my advice is to meet with at least three photographers. Try to get to know them a little and really check out their work.

When you're interviewing a potential photographer, do a comfort check. Are you relaxed with this person? Can you be yourself with them? Headshots are extremely personal. You need to like and trust your photographer.

And make sure they're listening to you. Communication is essential. Share all your fears and concerns. In my opinion, the best photographers will ask you as many questions as you ask them.

You also need to inspect their work. Do they shoot in a studio or do they work outdoors? I have no preference but you might. What about style? Are their shots natural or glamorous? These are all factors to consider.

Ethnic performers need to take special care. If you have dark skin, make sure the photographer has experience taking those kinds of pictures. The lighting concerns are very different. The same goes for extremely fair people with light blonde or red hair.

You should also give some thought to what time of day you would like to shoot. Some actors prefer mornings, others like afternoons. What works best for you? If the photographer can't accommodate your needs, cross his name off the list.

Some photographers forget that a headshot is a marketing tool, not a piece of art. I hate these people. Try and find someone who shoots headshots on a regular basis. They'll understand your goals better and they won't force their artistic vision on you.

"How much should I expect to pay?"

Okay, let's talk about price. Anything less than two hundred is a joke and anyone asking more than five hundred is a crook. Somewhere in the middle is just about right for good professional shots.

Keep in mind that most good photographers will offer to reshoot for no charge if you're not completely satisfied.

Getting a good headshot isn't cheap but it shouldn't empty out your bank account.

And finally, make sure you're ready for the big day. Taking headshots is work. So get a good night's sleep. You want to be rested for the shoot.

Some actors like to bring mood music to the studio. Others like to down a couple of beers first. Whatever works for you. Just find a way to enjoy the process.

You're probably thinking that finding the right photographer is a lot of work. Get over it. This is part of your job. Getting the right headshot is important and you don't want to make any mistakes.

Besides, once you're done, you probably won't have to go through this process again for at least a couple of years.

Resumes

Actors always spend a great deal of time and money to get the perfect headshot and then they attach it to a poorly done resume. It's important to remember that a great picture can be easily undermined by an unprofessional resume.

"I've seen many different types of acting resumes. Is there is particular format that's better?"

Despite variations in style and headings, most acting resumes are typically formatted the same way.

Your name and number always go on top, followed by any union affiliations. You can also include your height, weight, hair color and eye color. (Don't list your sizes and measurements; they belong on a commercial resume, not a theatrical one.)

After that, the credits are usually listed in the following order: film, television, theater, training, special skills. Why? I have no idea. For some reason, it's always done this way.

There's no need to be inventive with your resume. The layout is pretty standard and a creatively formatted resume will probably work against you.

Once you're done, print your resume on plain white paper. Color always looks childish to me. And when you attach it to your picture, please use staples, not paper clips. Your headshot and resume function as one and you don't want them to get separated.

On the opposite page is an example of a properly formatted resume.

AMY PARKER
SAG/AFTRA

Ht: 5'4"   Contact: 310/555-5555
Wt: 115 lbs
Hair: Blonde
Eyes: Blue

FILM

The Right Corner	Lead	UCLA Student Film
Audition	Supporting	AFI Student Film

TELEVISION

Gilmore Girls	Co-Star	WB/Dir: Lee Prentis
The West Wing	Featured	NBC/Dir: Bob Smith

THEATER

Hamlet	Ophelia	Old Globe Theater
The Seagull	Nina	Complex Theater
Jake's Women	Molly	Player's Space
Summer And Smoke	Nellie	Player's Space

TRAINING
Janet Alhanti — Meisner Technique
Bob Morrisey — Scene Study
Brian Reise — Cold Reading
TheaterSports — Improv

SPECIAL SKILLS
Most sports, horseback riding, surfing, great with animals.

Here are a few important don'ts:

DON'T list your home number and address on the resume. There's no way of knowing where that information is going to end up. I know plenty of young actresses who have been harassed because of this mistake.

DON'T include your social security number. That information is personal and in the world of identity theft, it is a serious mistake that could cause you a lot of grief.

DON'T be too specific. If you performed "Death of a Salesman" with some obscure theater company in Ohio, I don't need to know the director's name.

DON'T be overly creative. Blue eyes should be listed as blue, not aqua. And to this day, I have no idea what "flaxen hair" looks like.

DON'T make me think you're stupid. I'm talking about spelling. Being an actor shouldn't prevent you from being professional. Have someone proofread your resume.

And most importantly, **DON'T LIE!** Headshots are resumes are similar in the sense that they should both be honest and accurate.

"What do you look for on a resume?"

Let's assume you don't have tons of television and film credits. What else is going to catch my eye? Effort. That's right, effort. I want to see that you haven't been sitting around waiting for an agent to solve all your problems. You should be out there hustling your butt off so that when you do sign with an agency, you'll be ready to rock and roll.

So let's define effort. First, I look for it under the "Training" section of your resume. I'll ask myself, "Is this actor serious about his craft?" "Has he been training with a variety of teachers?" "Has he explored many different types of classes, including scene study, cold reading, voice, and movement?"

And again, don't even think about lying. If I'm really considering you as a client, I might call up your teacher and ask about your acting ability It sure would be embarrassing if he never heard of you.

I also look for effort under the "Theater" section. And this brings up one of my many pet peeves about actors. I'm constantly meeting actors who complain that they can't get any work because they don't have an agent. Bull! You may not be able to land a big guest star part on "Will and Grace", but you can definitely go out there and do some theater.

It depresses me when I meet an attractive, young actor who has never done one single play. Not only are they denying themselves a deeply satisfying performing experience, but they are also limiting their ability to grow as an actor.

If you're an actor, you should act. And yes, it is that easy. Acting is acting. It doesn't matter if you're doing community theater or working opposite Robert DeNiro. You need to practice your craft and build up your credits. Show me an extensive "Theater" section on a resume, and I'll show you an actor who loves acting.

Most of the established actors I represent are constantly complaining about being typecast. Theater gives you the freedom to play a variety of parts that you will rarely get a chance to perform as a working actor. Take advantage of that.

There's usually a "Special Skills" section at the bottom of an actor's resume. A lot of theatrical agents ignore this part but I find that it gives me a better sense of you as a person.

Always list skills that directly affect your acting and the roles you can play. This would include languages, dialects, musical skills and athletic ability. My advice is to keep it short and clean. You don't have to list every single sport you can play. Just put down "very athletic".

You should also list any skills that define you as a person. These don't have to be directly related to acting. What I'm looking for are little clues about you as an individual. I often find these items fascinating and they can provide interesting material for our first meeting.

Here are some of the cool special skills that have made me curious about a potential client:

Competitive Clam Shucking
Certified Phlebotomist
Amateur Contortionist
Psychic Channeling
Mocking Those in Authority
Former Navy Seal

But let me stress this one last time — don't lie! If we're sitting in my office and I notice that you've listed "ear wiggling" as a special skill, I'm going to ask you to do it. That's just the kind of guy I am.

Demo Reels

I have been working in this business for over ten years and I've never once had an actor not apologize for the quality of his demo reel. You guys always hand them over with a look of dread on your face. Sometimes I have to pry them out of your clenched fingers.

The truth is most actors who are just starting out don't have spectacular demo reels. Agents know that and it's no big deal. Our expectations about the tape will be based partly on your resume. If you don't have tons of credits, we're not going to expect scene after scene of you alongside major movie and TV stars.

You need to understand that agents watch tapes differently than you do. We're just trying to get a sense of how you photograph and what you've done. I've seen some pretty decent reels that were mostly commercials and bit roles. You'd be surprised at what you can put together with a just a little bit of creativity.

The key is to keep it short. The ideal demo reel should be under five minutes. Even if you have more work, don't feel that you have to include it all. Be selective. You run the risk of losing me if your reel is too long. I might love the first few scenes and then lose all interest if there's too much filler. So don't shoot yourself in the foot. More is not always better.

I once signed a young actor whose reel consisted of one single scene in a terrible low budget film. There was just something about him. Even the poor production quality couldn't hide it. After we started working together, I never used the reel again but it got him where he needed to be.

"What about trying to get work in a student film?"

Now there's a great idea. I think this is a fantastic way to collect material for your first reel.

Most of these kids are spending a fortune to produce their films and they're turning out really high quality work. After all, these movies are going to be their calling card to Hollywood so they have to be as professional as possible.

You're also getting a chance to meet future film-makers who might hire you when they hit it big.

The downside is that you're going to be working long hours for nothing more than a cheap meal and a pat on the back. That's cool because you're going to end up with some good footage for your first demo reel.

"But I've heard that actors always have trouble getting finished copies of student films."

Here's my advice. First, make sure you get contact numbers and addresses on all the filmmakers. You should also ask for their teacher's name. This information will come in handy if you have to track them down.

The next move is to sign a written agreement with the students. It should include the following information:

* A promise to provide you with a copy of the finished film.

* The approximate delivery date.

* An invitation to the first public screening.

Once everyone signs this agreement, make sure you send a copy to the teacher and the head of the film department.

If you're working for free, a copy of the finished film is your only compensation. If you behave like a professional, you shouldn't have any problems getting it.

You should take great pride in booking one of these films. The student who picks you is trusting you with his dreams. I think that's pretty impressive.

So get out there and audition for as many student films as you can. If nothing else, you'll get a chance to hone your auditioning skills.

"Can a bad reel hurt my chances of being signed?"

Absolutely. Sometimes, the material just isn't good enough. If that's the case, forget it. When you finally do sign with an agent, you'll get a chance to book more substantial work and then you'll be able to put together your first reel.

Don't Forget To Join SAG

In addition to all the tools we just talked about, it's very important that you join the union before you start looking for an agent.

LA is a union town. The majority of work available in film and television falls under the jurisdiction of the Screen Actors Guild, also known as SAG. So if you're not a member, you don't get to work.

If you live somewhere else and you're planning on relocating here, you should try to get in before you make the move. If that's not an option, make it one of your primary goals once you get here.

And don't assume your first agent will help you get a SAG card. That's not our job. To be honest, I have never signed anyone over the age of 25 who isn't already a union member.

At this point, I know what your next question is going to be. I can already hear it coming. "So how do I get a SAG card?"

That's easy. You just book a job.

"But you said it's impossible to book a job if you're not in SAG!"

Exactly. Isn't this fun?

Let's go to the horse's mouth. In their own words, here's how SAG explains what it takes to become a member:

"Generally, new members earn entrance into the Screen Actors Guild by meeting one of the following eligibility requirements:

1) Cast and hired to work in a principal or speaking role for a SAG signatory producer.

```
2) A minimum of one-year's membership
and principal work in an affiliated
performers' union, or...
```

```
3) Cast and hired to work in an extra
role for a SAG signatory producer at
full SAG rates and conditions for a
minimum of three work days."
```

Everybody got that? No? Okay, let's put it into English.

```
1) An actor must be cast and hired to
work in a principal or speaking role
for a SAG signatory producer.
```

In other words, you have to get a production company to "Taft-Hartley" you. This is a legal term that every new actor needs to understand.

According to federal Taft-Hartley laws, a non-union performer may work on a union shoot for up to 30 days, but after that, the actor must become a member of the union.

This means that if you can convince a casting director to hire you on a SAG project, then the production company will have to endorse you for union membership.

Most casting directors are hesitant to do this because unless you're a minor, it involves paying a fee and filing a lot of paperwork. Also, there are so many union actors in LA that it doesn't really make sense to go through the hassle.

On the other hand, if someone really wants you, they'll do whatever it takes to bring you on board. So while this isn't the easiest way to get into SAG, it can definitely be done when the circumstances are right.

This rule also applies to commercials. Commercial casting directors hire the best man for the job, union card or no union card. And once they book you, the door to SAG is wide open.

> 2) Performers may join SAG if the applicant is a paid-up member of an affiliated performers' union (ACTRAQ, AEAS, AFTRA, AGMA or AGVA) for a period of one year and has worked at least once as a principal performer in that union's jurisdiction.

This one sounds good but you have to read the language carefully. Being a member of other unions like AFTRA or Equity isn't enough. You have to be a *working* member.

> 3) An actor must be cast and hired to work in an extra role for a SAG sig-natory producer at full SAG rates and conditions for a minimum of three work days."

This is the most popular way to get into SAG. Unfortunately, the language is a little misleading. It sounds like all you have to do is work 3 days as an extra and you're in but that's not exactly true.

Here's the deal. Production companies hire union and non-union extras on every shoot. The assistant director is usually issued 3 vouchers, which he can hand out to 3 of the non-union extras.

When you collect 3 vouchers, then you can join SAG.

The problem is every non-union extra is gunning for one of those precious vouchers and they'll do anything to get it. The decision is made by the assistant director. It's completely up to him.

Needless to say, this is one popular guy.

Another factor to consider is the number of non-union extras on the set. It wouldn't make much sense to work in a concert scene with hundreds of other actors. What's the point? No one's going to notice you.

So be smart about doing extra work. Try to find projects where they only need a handful of people. That way, you increase your chances of getting a voucher.

And never list extra work on your resume. It's considered unprofessional and will mark you as a beginner.

NOTE: As this book goes to press, SAG has decided to update the voucher system. No one knows how long this will take but here's the information that I was given:

"SAG is currently revising the entrance for background performers by developing a point system in which union and non-union jobs, along with educational seminars and sanctioned events count toward professional experience."

"How much does it cost to join SAG?"

The initial fee is currently $1,310. This amount is payable in full at the time of application. After that, dues are based on your earnings under SAG contracts in the previous calendar year. So if you didn't make much last year, your dues will be fairly low.

And if money is tight, you don't have to join after your first job. At this point, you're considered "SAG Eligible", which is just as good. The union won't force you to become a member until you book a second job, then you're a "must join" and have to pay up *before* stepping foot on the set.

Check out SAG's website at www.SAG.org for more information on everything we've discussed.

Final Thoughts

I'm a professional and I like actors who behave like professionals. I have always been drawn to people who are serious about their careers.

I hate when actors come into my office for a meeting and tell me their new headshots aren't ready. Or that they haven't had time to edit their demo reels. This kind of behavior is always a red flag.

So go and gather your tools. They are ammunition for the coming battle to secure an agent. You should never approach me until you've got your act together.

Opportunity doesn't knock very often on the door of a struggling actor. But when it does, you want to be ready.

Getting
an
Agent

"An agent is a person who is sore because an actor gets 90% of what they make."

— Alva Johnson

Getting an Agent 4

"Okay — I'm in SAG, I've got a great picture, my resume looks good and I've put together a pretty decent demo reel. I'm also studying like crazy and I feel I'm ready to work. Now what?"

This is the hard part, gang. Getting an agent is very, very difficult. There just aren't enough of us to go around.

Here's a scary statistic. There are approximately 98,000 actors in the Screen Actors Guild and only 25% of them have agents. That explains the hundreds of submissions I receive on a monthly basis.

It also explains all the annoying phone calls I received at home when I first became an agent. The situation became so bad that I had to have my number unlisted.

Here's another scary statistic straight from SAG. "About 90% of our membership must rely on income outside of the acting profession for food and shelter." So we're talking about a union where most of the members would starve if they didn't have secondary sources of income.

Let's bottom-line it. If you want to start making a living, you need to get an agent in your corner. Assuming you're not kidding yourself and you really are talented, there are several ways to do it. And there are also several ways to screw it up.

Submissions

The most obvious way to get an agent's attention is to submit your picture and resume to the agency. Most actors assume this is a complete waste of time. Are they right?

Every day, talent agencies receive a ton of submissions from actors seeking representation. Envelope after envelope, filled with pictures and resumes, all from actors trying to land the right agent. Who the hell has time to open every one of those damn letters?

Well, the first thing you have to understand is that I open every single submission that lands on my desk. If my name is on the envelope, I'm going to open it and look inside. Why? Because you never know.

Years ago, I was going through the usual pile of submissions and was surprised to find a familiar face inside. It was an actor named Jack who had starred on several action shows during the nineties. His letter explained that he had taken time off to get married and start a family. Now he was ready to go back to work and on a whim, had done a blind mailing to a select group of agencies.

Naturally, I brought Jack in for a meeting and ended up signing him on the spot. Two months later, we heard that Paramount was putting together a new syndicated action show that was perfect for him. Calls were made and next thing you know, Jack is starring on his own show, which runs for three seasons and makes him a very wealthy man. The agency also collected a hefty commission on the deal. Why? Because we opened a blind submission.

You never know.

It takes almost no effort to open a submission and give it a quick look. It's a no brainer. Maybe I'm looking for an attractive young Asian actress to round out my list. Bang! There she is. Problem solved. And in Jack's case, those few seconds invested in opening his envelope paid off in a big way.

"Be honest. You recognized Jack from his work. Have you ever signed someone new from a blind submission?"

Yes. Many times. And that would hold true for most agents I know. Unfortunately, for every submission that leads to a meeting, I probably throw out hundreds of pictures. Should that prevent you from taking a shot? Of course not. When I say, you never know, it also applies to you.

I despise actors who are constantly whining about how hard it is to get an agent. You ask these doomsayers how often they send out their pictures and they typically respond that they stopped doing it. Why? "The odds are too great!" "I never get called in!" "It's a waste of time!"

Great attitude, huh? The only waste of time is sitting around being negative. No wonder these people can't get arrested as actors. They're always getting in their own way.

If you don't have an agent, you should be sending out your picture and resume at least five times a week. Five submissions a week, every week. It doesn't cost much and it certainly doesn't take that much time.

"Is there anything I can do to make my submission stand out?"

Absolutely. First, you should never mail your material to an agency without addressing it to a specific agent. This is a common actor mistake. If you don't make it out "Attention: Tony Martinez", it will stay in the agency's reception area with many, many others. Eventually, when hell freezes over, someone with free time will wander by and take a look.

It's much more efficient to target an individual agent. Anything with my name on it will end up on my desk. That makes it a little harder to ignore. The package will get opened. And that's half the battle.

Now, by the same token, you should NEVER do a blanket submission to every agent in the company. As we discussed earlier, a large part of my job is signing new clients. If I bring in an actor and one of the other agents books him on a film, I still get to commission part of that deal. I had nothing to do with it but I still see money because I'm responsible for that actor being a client. That's the incentive for us to sign new people.

So if you do a blanket submission and two agents are interested, you may think you're in a great spot, but you're not. You're screwed. Why? Because we're not going to fight over you. It's not worth it. Better to keep peace than start a conflict over a possible client.

The bottom line is pick one agent and send your submission to that person. If there's no response after a few weeks, then you can submit to someone else at the agency.

And please don't make your envelope impossible to open. I'm serious about this. You're not sending me a top-secret document; it's just a picture and resume. So don't glue the flap and then cover it with tape. Paper cuts tend to ruin my day and your chances of getting called in.

Here's a funny little story that illustrates why agents often lose patience with actors.

While I was working at Epstein Wyckoff, two agents were promoted and the company changed its name to Epstein, Wyckoff, Corsa, Ross and Associates. This new information was listed in all the directories that actors refer to when sending out their pictures.

The change was listed like this:

From now on, all submissions should be addressed to:

Epstein, Wyckoff, Corsa, Ross & Associates
Attn: Indicate Department
280 South Beverly Drive
Beverly Hills, CA 90212

During the next few weeks, we received over 40 submissions that were addressed to our Indicate Department. Can you believe that? That's like those old Abbott and Costello movies where the drill sergeant says, "Repeat after me. I, state your name" and Costello answers, "I, state your name".

As I've said before, I don't like lazy actors. It's not so much that there are people out there who don't know what the word "indicate" means. What bothers me is that they were too lazy to look it up before using the word in a business letter.

I always wanted to bring some of those clowns in for a meeting with my indicate department. I would ask them if they had any indicating experience and then watch them sweat their way through an answer. How much fun would that be? Sometimes there aren't enough hours in the day.

"When's the best time to look for an agent?"

Agents are always searching for talent. 24 hours a day, 7 days a week, 52 weeks a year. It's the one part of our job that we never put on hold.

But it's also wise to maximize your chances. That's how you win in Vegas. The best odds are always at the craps and blackjack table. Only suckers play roulette.

So I would say that May, June, and July are the best times to look for representation. Why? Because pilot season is over and every agency in town is rethinking their list.

Here's how it works. Most television pilots are cast between January and April. This is the time of year when we're all working long hours to book our clients on shows that might possibly end up on the air. There's a lot of money at stake and our focus tends to be very narrow during pilot season.

Once it's over, we catch our breath and start making changes on our lists. Actors that aren't generating money get dropped, creating room for new clients. As a result, we tend to be more open minded in the months that follow pilot season.

Also, you should never submit your material to an agent during December. The year is winding down, the holidays are upon us and we're all thinking about more important things — like pilot season.

"My friends say that if I write "Requested Material" on the envelope, it will trick agents into opening my submission. Is that true?"

Of course it's true. Most agents are as dumb as a box of hair. Those two words always manage to get the best of me.

In case you didn't catch it, I'm being sarcastic. I know exactly what I have requested from actors. If anything, when actors try to pull this con, it just makes me upset and the submission ends up getting tossed.

So write whatever you want. It makes absolutely no difference. If the package is addressed to me, it will get to me. End of story.

"Should I send agents an unsolicited demo reel?"

Every agent in the world will tell you not to. No one has time to see them and all those tapes tend to pile up quickly. If an agent wants to see your tape, he will ask for it.

That's how agents always answer this question. Hell, that's how I always answer this question. But you didn't buy this book to hear the same old company line, right? You want the truth.

In my opinion, the answer is a resounding YES! Why not? The truth is that it's very easy to throw out a picture and resume. But despite all my complaining, I don't think I've ever thrown out a reel without watching it first.

"I've heard actors sometime attach their submissions to weird little gifts. Does that work?"

Years ago, every agent in town received the same submission. It was a box with a picture and resume attached to it. Inside, there was a human foot. Not a real one, but an exact copy, the kind you'd find in a doctor's office.

The note said "I'm just trying to get my foot in the door".

Funny, right? Everyone I know still remembers that submission. But as far as I know, no one ever signed the actor.

Gimmicks don't work.

Food is a bad idea too. Over the years, I've had actors attach their submission to pizza boxes, muffin baskets and breakfast trays. The other agents always devour this stuff. But I never do. No way.

Call me paranoid but I don't want to go down in history as the first Hollywood agent to be poisoned by an angry actor.

"What about the cover letter? Do agents actually read them?"

Nope. We can't be bothered. Who has time? But that doesn't mean you shouldn't include one. My advice is to keep it short and sweet. You should also type it. Handwritten letters always seem unprofessional. To me, an unprofessional letter equals an unprofessional actor.

And please don't compare yourself to celebrities. Here's the way one actress described herself in a recent cover letter:

"I possess the quirky aloofness of a Renee Zellweger, the sensibility and looks of a Hope Davis, and the commitment, drive and flair of a young Meryl Streep."

Okay, what exactly does any of that mean?

I've also seen all the funny letters that are out there and after a while, they become very tedious. For example — "David Letterman's Top Ten Reasons You Should Represent Me". I've gotten plenty of those.

It's rare but every now and then, someone surprises me with a truly original cover letter. Here's an example of one that I actually kept. It's from an actress named Ellen:

INT. TONY'S OFFICE — DAY

TONY MARTINEZ, a handsome and powerful talent agent, is seated behind his desk. He's in the middle of a telephone conversation.

> TONY
> I know you're the head of NBC
> but I just can't help you. I don't
> represent any young women with
> red hair who are good at comedy.
> Sorry.

Depressed, he hangs up and throws his headset across the room.

> TONY
> God, what am I going to do???

Just then, the door opens and an attractive young woman with bright red hair walks in. Her name is ELLEN.

                    ELLEN
        Hi, I'm your four o'clock meeting.

Ellen trips and does a pratfall. Tony's eyes open wide. He jumps out of his seat...

                    TONY
        You're exactly what I'm looking
        for!!!

I laughed out loud when I first read this letter. So did everyone in my office. Impressed, I took a meeting with Ellen and ended up referring her to a friend at a smaller agency who signed her on the spot.

The truth is that when I glance at a cover letter, I am looking for one thing and one thing only. The very first sentence should say, "My name is and I was referred to you by..."

That leads us to the single most valuable weapon in your quest to get a meeting with an agent.

Referrals

I never, ever ignore referrals. If someone in the business asks me to meet an actor, I'll do it. It's a matter of respect. And now that I've done that person a favor, I can ask them to do something for me. That's what keeps the wheels spinning here in Hollywood.

Now, the first rule about referrals is that they have to be real. You can't just make them up. If you say that a casting director suggested you contact me, I will give that person a call to confirm your statement. And he damn well better know you. If he doesn't, you have now pissed off an agent AND a casting director. Not a good idea.

The second rule is that the person has to actually pick up the phone and call me. If an acting teacher tells you it's ok to use her name in your cover letter, that's not good enough. Sorry. It's too easy. The teacher is probably just being nice to you. She has to go the extra mile and contact me directly. She really needs to put herself and her reputation on the line.

Why? Remember when I said that agents are judged by who they represent? Referrals work the say way. Everyone in show business is judged by who they endorse. If someone refers an idiot to me, then that person becomes an idiot too.

Did you ever see the movie "Donnie Brasco"? There's a scene where Pacino introduces Johnny Depp to his mob friends. He makes a point of saying "this is a friend of mine". In other words, he is saying that this guy can be trusted because he's endorsing him.

The entertainment industry is the same way. So if someone is serious about helping you out with a referral, they have to contact me directly. There's no other way.

Keep in mind that a referral doesn't always have to be from someone in the industry. I get calls from friends all the time. The conversation usually starts with, "you probably hate when people do this but I know an actor who's looking for an agent and I was thinking..."

Sure, I'll meet the actor. Why not? That's what friends are for. I've taken meetings based on referrals from friends, lovers, doctors, and even my mom. They're not as valuable as a professional referral but once you're in the door, you never know what might happen.

Besides, I ain't saying no to mom.

Assistants

Another good strategy is to target an assistant. Assistants are the backbone of this business. They work extremely hard for very little pay, hoping that at some point, they will get a chance to move up the food chain.

Assistants are an agent's first line of defense against the hordes of actors who are seeking representation. That makes them your best friend or your worst nightmare. It's up to you.

My assistant has complete access to me. If he refers an actor, I will usually take a meeting with that person. On the other hand, if he tells me you were rude on the phone, I will never take your call.

When I was training, I often kept track of actors that I thought were talented. And when I became an agent, I looked up some of those people and they became my clients.

Here's a great story that might inspire you. An actress named Susan sent me her picture while I was still an assistant at Paradigm. She didn't have much experience but there was definitely something unique about her look. The photographer had really earned his money. So instead of tossing it, I kept her submission.

Flash forward nine months and I'm working as an agent at Epstein Wyckoff. As I move into my new office, I happen to come across Susan's picture. On a whim, I give her a call and it turns out she's still looking for representation.

So the two of us meet and I end up signing her. A few weeks later, she books a nice supporting role in the Tom Cruise film "Jerry McGuire"!

You never know.

So always, always treat assistants with respect. They can be valuable allies in your quest for representation.

Performing

Actors who are looking for an agent always ask me the same question:

"Do you like to go see plays?"

I usually laugh because this is a very misleading question. What they really want to know is:

"Is there any chance you'll come see me in a play?"

See the difference? The first thing actors need to learn is that theater is not a means to an end. The play itself is the reward, not a phone call from an agent.

So if you're going to do a play, make sure you do it for the right reason. Your goal should be to put on good work and grow as an actor, not to be discovered or seen by industry types. Should that happen, great! Good for you. But if it doesn't, you have a little more experience now, which will help you be ready when opportunity comes knocking on your door.

That said, yes, I love going to the theater. I never have to pay so for me, it's a cheap date. Unfortunately, many agents in LA really hate plays. Why? Because there's a lot of bad theater in this town.

> "I will accept anything in the theater, provided it amuses or moves me. But if it does neither, I want to go home."
>
> — Noel Coward

Actors in Hollywood are obsessed with success and that isn't very conducive to good theater. Why worry about creating great drama when you can book a few scenes on "24"?

On that note, here are some suggestions for increasing the odds of getting me to show up at your show:

1) If you're going to do theater in LA, make sure you do it in LA. I won't drive more than half an hour to see a show. Now, if you want to send a limo to pick me up, that's a whole other story.

2) Make sure you pick a safe neighborhood I'm serious about this. Choose a theater that's easy to find with plenty of secure parking. I can't enjoy your work if I'm worried about getting home alive.

3) If it's warm out, make sure the air conditioner is working. I can't tell you how many hours I've spent sitting in the dark, sweating like a pig. (And please don't turn it off during the show! If an actor can't project above the gentle hum of an air conditioner, then he has no business being on stage.)

4) One-man shows suck. Sorry. There's no other way to say it. So unless you're Eric Bogosian or Ann Magnunson, stay away from these narcissistic productions! You have to be exceptionally talented and experienced to pull one off.

5) On the same point, agents respond to larger casts. A production with seven characters allows me to scout seven actors. That's much better than two. (And more parts mean more actors working to get industry people to show up!)

"So how exactly do you choose which play you're going to see?"

Usually, it depends on who's in it. Clients and friends get top priority. After that, it's based on word of mouth, reviews and the all mighty referral. Then there are times when an actor will send me a flyer that looks intriguing and I'll go check it out on a whim.

Let me remind you again that inviting an agent's assistant to your show is a fantastic idea. They love scouting talent for their bosses and their own future client lists. If my assistant mentions that he went to a play, I always ask if there was anyone good in it.

When a play comes together, it's a wonderful thing to behold. When it doesn't, it's like having root canal done but it takes longer. So choose the material wisely. Make sure you have something to say. And then surround yourself with the most talented cast and crew that you can find.

Good luck!

The Comedy Scene

Reader's Digest said it best — laughter is the best medicine. Is there anyone out there who doesn't enjoy a good comedy? The ability to make someone laugh is priceless.

Agents are always searching for hot new talent on the comedy scene. The same holds true for casting directors. We all want to discover the next Jim Carrey.

Personally, I love actors who are funny. I grew up watching Charlie Chaplin movies and I still feel the first five years of Saturday Night Live will never be topped. So if you can make me laugh, you're half way home.

There are three ways to go here:

STAND-UP COMEDY

Frankly, I'm not a big fan. It's been my experience that most comedians cannot act. That's why for every show like "Seinfeld", there are tons of others that never make it.

Standing on stage doing a routine doesn't mean you can interact with other actors. It's not the same thing. Then again, I know at least three agents who disagree with me. Take that how you will.

If you decide to try stand-up, the best clubs are "The Comedy Store", "The Improv" and "Laugh Factory". Industry types are often present and all three have open mike nights.

SKETCH COMEDY

This is the stuff you see on "Saturday Night Live" and "Mad TV". If you're able to create a wild mix of characters, then this is the world for you.

Agents are always scouting sketch shows because these actors have unlimited potential. The best places to study and perform are "The Groundlings", "Second City" and "The ACME Comedy Theater".

Sketch comedy isn't for everyone but if you can do it, there are plenty of agents out there who will want to meet you.

IMPROV

This is a very dangerous form of comedy. Actors are up on stage without a script, working off audience suggestions. There's no safety net. All they have is their training and each other.

I love improvisers because their skills translate into all forms of acting and they can usually handle anything you throw at them. This talent can also be helpful in landing a commercial agent because most commercial auditions are usually improvised.

There are plenty of groups out there like "TheatreSports", "Improv Olympic" and "The LA Connection" who will train you in this unique art form.

Showcases

Another way to attract an agent's attention is through the magic of "showcasing". In basic terms, a showcase usually features a large group of actors performing a series of short scenes for an audience of industry guests. They usually take about an hour and feature a wide range of material and performers. Some are produced in a theater; others are done in a studio.

Performing in a scene showcase is a popular way to meet an agent. I tend to enjoy these because it gives me an opportunity to see a large group of actors in a short period of time. Also, if one of the scenes isn't very good, there's another one right around the corner.

And this works both ways. I may get to see a lot of potential clients but, if attendance is good, you get to perform for more than one agent or casting director. That means if I don't respond to your work, the guy next to me might.

Many acting schools and theater companies produce showcases as a way of exposing their members to the industry. I've also been to showcases that are put together by groups of actors who rent a space and do all the work themselves.

Either way, you're not alone. You have a large group of people working as a team to attract as many agents and casting directors as possible. There's strength in numbers and this will obviously work to your advantage.

The trick here is getting people to actually show up. So if you decide to do a showcase, you'll need to become the ultimate publicist. It takes hard work to put butts in those seats but like I said before, at least you're not alone.

Showcases are always held in the evening, after work, on week nights. The best time is right at 7:30. That gives us plenty of time to get there.

Showcases are never, ever held on weekends or Friday nights. I'm sure you can figure out why.

And don't forget what I said earlier about assistants! If you can't get an agent to attend, definitely target the support staff.

When I was an assistant, I loved being invited to showcases and plays. It made me feel like I was important too and as a result, I was probably a lot more receptive than many of the agents around me.

Paid Showcases

There's another type of showcase that's worth mentioning. For lack of a better term, let's call them "paid showcases".

There are many companies in LA that for a fee, act as a middleman between actors and the entertainment industry. They produce showcases in their own private studios and they give an honorarium to the industry guests for their time.

Here's how it works. Actors pay a fee to be part of the showcase and in return, all you have to do is show up and perform your scene. You also get to participate in a question and answer period with the agent or casting director. It can be a one-time deal or you can sign up for a series of showcases.

Some of the larger and more respected companies like "TVI" and "AIA" offer a wide variety of choices. For example, you can sign up for a series of showcases that target specific types of casting directors, like ones who work on soap operas or others who only cast sitcoms.

In my opinion, paid showcases are a viable way to make solid connections and gather important information. The seminar format provides an opportunity to interact and network with fellow actors, agents, casting directors and other industry professionals.

These companies also save you the hassle of having to produce your own evening of scenes and trying to get people to show up. That way, you can focus on the acting, not organizing and promotion.

And for the record, yes, I have signed several actors from places like "AIA" and "TVI", actors that I never would have met otherwise.

"When I'm performing at a showcase, is it better to do a scene or a monologue?"

I hate monologues. There are plenty of agents that disagree with me but they're wrong. I, for one, have never understood the appeal of a monologue. I think there's something very artificial about watching a performer interact with an unseen character.

I have never, ever signed an actor based on his work in a monologue and I never will. A good monologue might give me a sense of your ability but I need much more information before I can consider representing you. Show me an agent who signs an actor off a monologue and I'll show you an agent who knows nothing about acting.

Here's the problem. Acting is about reacting. As an agent, I need to see how you work with another performer. What's your timing like? Can you be in the moment? When the other actor is speaking, are you listening or are you just waiting to say your next line? Monologues don't give you a chance to address any of these concerns.

I once saw a guy do a pretty decent romantic monologue but when I asked him to do a scene with an actual woman, he wasn't able to generate any real chemistry.

And the last time I checked, every professional film or TV audition involves you acting out a scene with a casting director. Let's count. That's two people. Together. Creating a moment. See what I'm saying?

That said, fine, you've decided to ignore me. You're going to try a monologue anyway. Great. It's your funeral. But I will give you two crucial pieces of advice.

The first one is — don't sit in a chair.

For some unknown reason, actors love to perform their entire monologues while sitting in a chair. I've never understood this.

Unless the piece specifically calls for it, you shouldn't glue your butt to a chair. It's a very low status choice and it's hard to command attention when you're not standing.

At the very least, you can sit for part of the piece but at some point, you're going to have to get up and take charge.

Chairs may seem like harmless pieces of furniture but in actuality, they're evil monsters that suck the energy out of monologues.

The second piece of advice is — don't make eye contact with me!

You should direct the monologue to an abstract point in the back of the studio or better yet, have another actor sit off the side. At least that way, you have someone to focus on.

I remember going to a showcase where a woman performed an incredibly angry monologue about a man who had broken her heart. She decided to use me for eye contact.

What a stupid decision. It wasn't a lot of fun for me to sit there while she screamed on and on about how I had ruined her life. Instead of thinking about her acting, I just kept hoping she would shut up.

Keep this in mind — I cannot observe your scene if you make me part of it.

"I get it. You don't like monologues. Any advice on picking a scene?"

First off, pick a contemporary piece. If we end up working together, you will usually be auditioning for projects that take place in this century. Ibsen and Shakespeare were great writers but that's not what I need to see.

Actors sometimes ask if I prefer comedy or drama. That's completely up to you. If you're funny, go for it. If you're not, don't take the chance. You only get one shot to make an impression.

Next, make sure it's a role that you would be cast in. Simple, right? You'd be surprised at how many actors screw this one up. I once had a little guy with toothpick arms pick a scene where he had to play a mob enforcer.

So be realistic. Consider your type and age. Then ask yourself, is this a role that someone would really hire me to play?

You should also keep it short. More is not better. Hit me hard and hit me fast. I generally know within the first 60 seconds if I'm interested. No scene should ever be longer than five minutes.

Here's something else to consider. <u>DON'T</u> do scenes from famous movies. You will only suffer by comparison.

Young actors always pick the scene from "Good Will Hunting" where Matt Damon and Minnie Driver have the big fight.

This is such a bad idea. I always end up thinking how much better the actual actors were in the film. Don't set yourself up for failure by competing with movie stars.

"Let's say you saw me perform in a showcase. If I don't hear from you right away, does that mean you didn't like my work?"

Not necessarily. Agents pass on actors for a variety of reasons, many of which have nothing to do with talent.

Here are the top three reasons why I would not sign a good actor:

1 — **Marketability** is a big issue. An actor might be talented but I still have to figure out if I can sell him. The answer to that question can be determined by age, type, experience, and the needs of the casting community. Remember, this is a business. Agencies survive

by representing actors who are not only talented, but are capable of generating income.

2 — **Conflicts** are also a consideration. A client list is a delicate thing. If it's too small, it won't be able to meet my casting needs. And if it's too large, it becomes hard to service and clients end up not getting enough attention. So if I have too many actors who are just like you (in terms of age and type), I will not take you on too. You're a "conflict". And if I did sign you, I wouldn't be able to give you enough attention and your presence would take valuable time away from my current clients.

3 — **Lack of passion** is last but not least. I rarely sign an actor just because they're talented. There has to be something else. I have to be excited. Something about that person has to make me feel passionate enough to represent them.

Now, if I see a talented actor in a showcase but decide that for whatever reason I can't sign them right away, I won't just throw out their picture and resume. I'm not an idiot. What I will do is keep their information on file. Like most agents, I have an excellent system for tracking talent that I might like to represent in the future.

If you fall into this category, I might call you after a showcase and tell you that I enjoyed your acting but this isn't the right time for us to work together. I'll usually ask you to stay in touch and keep me informed of any advances in your career.

Now here's the amazing part. Very few actors ever take me up on that offer. They just drop off the face of the planet and I never hear from them again.

Which is just fine with me. If you can't recognize an open door when you see it, then you probably have no future in this business anyway.

There's one last thing I want you to always remember. The sad truth of every agent's life is that we cannot represent every talented actor we meet. It's just not possible. If we did, our client lists would number in the thousands and we would never be able to service and sell all those people.

So we have to pick and choose. And yes, sometimes we make mistakes. But at the end of the day, all we have is our professional judgment.

Keep that in mind the next time an agent passes on you.

Final Thoughts

One of the biggest misconceptions about agents is that we don't like actors. This isn't true. It would be impossible to do our job if we didn't like actors. We just don't like some of the things you guys do to get our attention.

I was once in a bar having a drink with my former assistant Heather. We had become good friends and were catching up on our lives. Anyone who didn't know us would have thought we were a couple on a date, having a good time.

Anyway, I excused myself to go to the bathroom and while I'm standing at the urinal, someone taps me on the shoulder. I turn around and it's this actor I passed on over a year ago.

He starts to explain how he's grown and how I should seriously reconsider working with him. While he's pitching me, I wash my hands and mumble something about sending a picture and resume to my office.

Pretty awkward, right? Wait. It gets better.

I go back to my table and start talking to Heather again. All of a sudden, the same actor walks over and without being invited, he sits down and joins us. The guy starts pitching himself again until I finally have to ask him to leave.

Besides the unprofessional behavior, this actor also made another big mistake. He mentioned the name of his manager who happened to be a friend of mine.

So the next day, I called up the manager and told him about his client's lack of manners. I explained how it reflected badly on him. Sure enough, the manager ended up firing the annoying actor.

This story shows why it's important to approach agents in a professional manner with all your tools in place. It lets us know that you understand how the game is played and the knowledge only adds to your value as a potential client.

The
All
Important
<u>Meeting</u>

"Be prepared for luck."

— Robin Williams

The All Important Meeting 5

Congratulations! You did it. You managed to get my attention and I've agreed to take a meeting. That means you get one shot to convince me that my career as an agent cannot continue unless your name is on my list.

The process is simple. First, I always meet one on one with potential clients. This gives me a chance to really get to know the person.

If that goes well, I ask the actor to come back and meet the other agents. It's essential that everyone be in agreement. One agent should never try to convince the others to sign someone.

And that's basically it. The only problem is actors tend to be their own worst enemy. Believe it or not, actors seeking representation are always convincing me NOT to sign them.

Pretty depressing, right?

I'm always amazed by how much effort actors put into getting a meeting with me but none of you ever know how to behave once you're actually in my office.

It's happened countless times. I'll start a meeting with an open mind, and then 15 minutes later, you couldn't pay me to work with that person.

So let's talk about all the things that can go wrong once you're actually in my office.

Bad Meetings

Before we tackle this subject, let's make something clear. *I want to like you.* It's my job to sign actors and if you're sitting in my office, that means you did something right.

Maybe I noticed your submission. Maybe someone referred you. Or maybe I saw your work in a showcase. Whatever it was, something positive happened to get your butt into that chair. So don't turn that positive into a negative. You've got 15 minutes to make an impression. That's 900 seconds. You have to use that time wisely.

"So what's the biggest mistake actors make in a meeting?"

Meeting with an agent is like a first date. You've got two people in a room. They're sizing each other up. And they're both wondering if it's going to go any further.

So ask yourself this: what's the worst thing you can do on a first date?

Answer: Talk about yourself.

There's nothing worse than being stuck on a date with someone who spends the whole night going on and on about themselves. It's the same thing in a meeting. I tend to tune out actors who waste their time by doing a non-stop monologue about who they are and what they want.

So don't play into the stereotype of the narcissistic, self-involved actor. It's dull. It's boring. And worst of all, it doesn't give me a chance to really get to know you.

And while we're on this point, I hate name droppers. I'm talking about actors who love to mention all the famous people they know, as if that's going to impress me.

An actress once dropped Matthew Perry's name a total of five times during our meeting. I couldn't believe it. To this day, she still holds the record.

A similar mistake actors often make is that they sit there and tell me about all the stuff on their resume. Don't you realize that I've already seen your resume? The odds are I'm holding it in my hands while we talk. I'm not a shy guy. If I have any questions, I'll ask.

"I've always been told that I should be ready to pitch myself to agents."

Boy, talk about lousy advice. Whoever told you that should be shot. You have to understand that I sell for a living. A large part of my job is pitching clients to casting directors. So the last thing I need is for an actor to come in and spend 15 minutes doing a half-assed pitch.

Here are some of the annoying pitches I've heard in meetings, followed by what I was really thinking:

"If you get me out there, I'll book."
(Don't make promises you can't keep.)

"I'm a loyal guy. When I make it, I won't leave you for a larger agency."
(You're a big fat liar.)

"I just know I'm going to be famous!"
(I wonder who's on Letterman tonight.)

These are just a few examples that demonstrate why you should leave the pitching to me. I'm much better at it. Which is why you want me to sign you, right?

At this point in my career, I would be thrilled if an actor came in and said, "If you sign me, I promise to do the best that I can and not embarrass you too badly."

Now there's a pitch.

"Great. After all that, there's no way I can go into a meeting without being nervous. What about the old Hollywood expression — never let them see you sweat?"

Don't worry about being nervous. Most agents are people too. We know that meetings can be stressful and we allow for that. If anything, I usually go out of my way to help actors relax. It makes for a better meeting all around.

And it's okay to ask for a glass of water.

"Do you have any advice on how to dress for a meeting?"

What can I say? Just be yourself. Wear comfortable clothes that will allow you to relax during the meeting And don't try to create any false impressions. Give me a chance to get to know the real you.

In all honesty, I can only remember one instance where an actress ruined her chances of being signed by wearing the wrong outfit.

The story involves a well known client who had accepted a part in a low budget movie There was no money in it but he got to play a character that was well outside his safety zone.

Unfortunately, the film was never released. My client wanted me to see his work so he arranged a private screening. I braced myself for the worst but you know what? The movie was great. I really enjoyed it.

In addition to that, the lead actress caught my eye. She was pretty in a quiet way and her performance carried the film. According to my client, this was her first real acting job.

Ready for the kicker? I watched the film on a Monday night and the following morning, I received a headshot from her in the mail. Just like that. And she had no idea that I had seen the film and represented the lead. They hadn't spoken in ages.

Now, you have to understand that I'm one of those people that find meaning in every action. I believe that things happen for a reason. Six months had passed since the film wrapped and this girl just happens to send me her picture the day after I've watched it?

That's a million to one shot, folks. We were obviously meant to work together.

So I called her in for a meeting and I have never been so embarrassed in my life. She showed up wearing a tiny little dress with no underwear. The word "slutty" doesn't even begin to describe this outfit. She was literally falling out of it.

At the time, I was working at an agency where my office was at the far end of a long row of other offices, each with an assistant stationed outside. I was later told that every single employee stopped what they were doing to watch this girl bounce down the hall, every step threatening to knock loose one of her breasts.

The other agents goofed on me for the rest of the day. One of them even left an ad for an escort service on my desk.

The worst part is that she was very sweet and likeable during the meeting. Her appearance didn't match her personality. Someone had obviously told her that she had to show off the goods to get an agent in Hollywood.

Bad advice. I still thought she was a great actress but there was no way I could sell her to the other agents. Even if I had forced the issue, no one was going to take her seriously.

So what can I say? Just be yourself. Dress like you always do. Give me a chance to get to know the real you.

"It sounds like agent meetings are a lot like job interviews."

That's absolutely true. I am sizing you up from the moment you walk in the door. Everything you do and say will factor into my decision about representing you.

I recently met an actress who had booked the lead in a film that went straight to video. This was pretty impressive because she didn't have much experience. I was seriously thinking about signing her.

As the meeting was ending, I asked her to leave her tape and she handed me a copy of the entire two hour movie. When I asked why she hadn't cut together an actual reel, the actress explained that she hadn't gotten around to it yet.

I decided to press her on the point because the movie had been finished for almost eight months. And that's when she cut her own throat. The actress told me she was lazy by nature. That's why she needed a good agent.

Excuse me? Like I said before, actors are very skilled at getting in their own way.

"Anything else I should avoid?"

There are two human traits that will always turn me off during a meeting. They are ANGER and DESPERATION. These two emotions are not your friends. Stay away from them at all costs.

If you walk into my office, reeking of desperation, I'm not going to sign you. If you show up with an attitude, I'm not going to sign you. If you do *anything* to piss me off, I'm not going to sign you.

Got it?

I remember once seeing an actress doing really good work in a play and inviting her in for a meeting. I was in a perfectly good mood that lovely spring day, feeling that all was right in the world.

Then this horrible woman walked into my office.

She had to be the angriest actor in Hollywood. She went on and on about how hard it was to get a damn agent and how she just couldn't catch a break. She cursed every agent who had passed on her and swore that one day, they would all be sorry.

Guess what? I didn't sign her.

I actually spent most of the meeting wondering what I would do if she pulled a gun. Anger is not an attractive quality. If you disagree, seek professional help.

Then there was the time I met with an actor I had seen perform in an improv show. The guy was funny but I was still on the fence about signing him. The decision could go either way.

Halfway through the meeting, he told me that we had met several years ago. It turns out I passed on him when I was working at another agency.

I was very surprised to hear this. I honestly didn't remember him. But he definitely remembered me. The guy was really upset that I hadn't signed him back then. We actually ended up getting into an argument over it.

Both of these examples support my theory that actors can be their own worst enemy.

In the first story, the woman was so furious about not being able to get representation, that she completely missed the fact that she was meeting with an agent who was seriously thinking about signing her.

And in the second story, why did the actor choose to remind me of a negative memory that I had already forgotten? If he could've just let go of the past (and his pride), all his problems might have been solved right then and there!

"I can't take much more of this. Do you have any positive stories?"

Yes, young Skywalker. We are finished with the dark side. Let's talk about...

Good Meetings

When meeting with an agent, you have to walk into that office and create an atmosphere where you can both get to know each other as people.

I have to forget that you're an actor seeking representation. That's boring. Instead, I need to see you as an individual. I have to get a sense of who you really are outside the world of show business.

How do you do this? Easy. Try to have a normal conversation. Maybe there's something in my office that catches your eye. Or maybe you just saw a great movie. Whatever. The idea is to get into a give and take situation where you're talking about anything but acting. This will give me a chance to get to know the real you.

And that's a two way street. Make an effort to get to know me too. Ask questions. Don't expect me to be interested in you if you show no interest in me.

Here are some examples of meetings that went really well.

I remember an actor who asked me why I liked being an agent. He thought it was a tough job where you're constantly dealing with people who want something from you. I didn't disagree but I did explain that there's a fun side too. This led to a great conversation about the business without talking directly about him.

This is a good meeting.

A potential client had just gotten back from a vacation in New Orleans, which happens to be one of my favorite cities. We ended up giving each other tips on the best dive bars in the French Quarter.

Another good meeting.

I once met with a young lady who had "tarot card reader" listed on her resume under Special Skills. It just so happens that I love anything having to do with the occult. So we started talking about it and the next thing you know, we're both sitting on the floor and she's giving me a reading. As a result, we really got to know each other and I ended up representing her for many years.

Now that's a great meeting. Especially for her.

"What else can I do to insure that a meeting goes well?"

When I first became an agent, I would try to sign established actors without knowing a lot about them. I never bothered to research their personal history. I just figured the strength of my pitch would be enough to persuade them to sign on as my client.

Was that a mistake? You're damn right it was. And it's a mistake that actors make all the time.

A lot of actors I meet tend to come across with a sense of self-entitlement. They act as if the business owes them something. "I'm here. I'm talented. Isn't that enough?"

The answer is no.

Gathering information is a huge part of your job. How can you go into a meeting with an agent and not know anything about that person or their company?

So do your homework. Ask everyone you know about the agency. And don't tell me you don't have enough contacts. That's bull. You're just being lazy.

Try using the "six degrees of separation" theory. Maybe someone in your class knows someone who is dating an actor who is roommates with a client at that agency. If you make an effort, you'll be surprised at how easy it is to gather information.

In short, you need to do the necessary homework that might give you that extra edge. And if you don't, trust me, someone else will.

"What kind of questions do you ask in a meeting?"

I usually start with, "how's it going" and then I allow the actor to set the tone. If you're a little nervous, I might ask where you're from in an attempt to get the meeting going.

But don't expect me to pull teeth. You're an actor. You should be prepared to do some talking. It's not that hard. Start with a noun and verb, then throw me some adjectives.

Now, despite everything I said, I will bring up some professional matters. I'll usually ask the following three questions:

1. Have you ever had an agent?
2. Do you have any auditioning experience?
3. Are you meeting with any other agents and if so, who?

Keep in mind there are no wrong answers to these questions. I'm just trying to get a sense of where you are in your career. So answer honestly and don't worry about what I'm thinking.

Here's another of my pet peeves. If I ask about your goals, please don't tell me you just want to work. I like actors who have given some thought to their careers. A new client once told me that her goal was to book one major guest star role inside of three months.

Now that's my kind of answer.

"Just curious. Have you ever made any mistakes during a meeting?"

A few years ago, one of the other agents at my office set up a meeting with an actress named Kelly. He was very excited about her and was hoping that we'd all agree to sign her.

From the moment she walked in, I was hit with an overpowering feeling that I knew her from someplace. I just couldn't figure out where.

So the meeting starts and I'm the only one not saying anything. I'm just sitting there, staring at this
woman, trying to figure out how I know her.

And then it hit me.

Have you ever blurted something out? Sometimes,
a thought pops into your head and before you know
it, the words are coming out of your mouth. And
there's not a damn thing you can do to stop it.

That's what happened here. The circuit breaker in
my brain must've been fried because right then and
there, in the middle of a business meeting, I shouted
out:

"I've seen you naked!"

All the other agents did a double take. Kelly
looked like she had been slapped. And I closed my
eyes, wishing I could turn back time.

It turns out that six months ago, I had seen Kelly
in a production of the David Mamet play "Edmond".
She had to perform an extended nude scene and I
guess it made an impression.

I know, I know — going to the theater isn't like
going to a strip club but you have to understand that
this was a small building and I was sitting right in the
first row. Get the picture?

So after I apologized ten thousand times, we all
had a good laugh and the agency ended up representing her. It's a good thing she had a sense of humor.

"When a meeting is over, what's the first thing you consider?"

First and foremost, I always ask myself, did I like that person? Would I enjoy working with him?

The truth is I have passed on plenty of talented actors simply because they fell under the category of "life is too short". Sometimes you just know that someone has unrealistic expectations or that they're going to be more trouble than they're worth.

I can't tell you how many life-altering decisions have been made based on whether or not an agent likes someone.

I remember once sitting in a staff meeting discussing a potential client. We were going back and forth on what to do until the owner said, "Well, this kid doesn't have much experience but I have to say, he seemed like a really good guy. What the hell? Let's take a chance."

And just like that, the actor found himself a home. Why? Because in addition to being talented, he was also very likeable. Decisions are made this way all the time at every agency in town.

Performing Scenes in Offices

One of the first things they teach you in agent school is never, ever sign an actor unless you've seen their work. That means you can't go on word of mouth. You have to watch that person's reel or you have to see them perform live. It's hard to be convincing when you're pitching an actor you've never actually seen act.

So let's say you've had a great meeting with an agent and now he wants to see your work. Or maybe he's already seen your work and now he wants the other agents to see it too. The bad news is you don't have a demo reel. So what are your choices?

Well, you're going to have to do a scene in the office. This is a tough one, folks. I can't tell you how many times I've seen actors do great work at a showcase, and then when I bring them in to do the exact same scene in my office, they completely tank.

There's no excuse for this because film and TV auditions are always held in a casting director's office. If you can't perform your scene in an office, it just warns me that you're not ready to audition. And if you're not ready to audition, why should I sign you?

Here are some suggestions that might help you perform a successful scene. Please learn from the mistakes of your fallen comrades.

1) **Don't Smoke**. Most offices are closed environments where the windows don't open. Blowing second hand smoke in my face is not a good idea. The funny part is that scenes never start with someone smoking. If they did, I could just put the brakes on right away. But no. Actors always pull out the cigarette at the halfway point, when I just don't feel right about interrupting the scene. So instead, I just have to sit there, dreaming up really cool ways to kill them.

2) **No Liquids**. Trust me. No matter how much you rehearse, you're going to end up spilling. I remember one brilliant actor who popped open a beer bottle which had been shaken too much. It was like a Budweiser bomb had gone off. Needless to say, we did not sign him.

3) **Avoid Props**. Unless it's absolutely necessary, do not use props. They take forever to set up and something always goes wrong. This goes double for prop guns. If you really must use one, tell the agents first. Show it to them. Put everyone's mind at ease. And even then, no matter how much you want to, don't point the gun at the agents.

4) **No Sex**. An office is a very small space. We're all on top of each other. If you and your partner start getting intimate, it creates a really weird vibe. Suddenly, the scene isn't about acting; it's about two people making out in front of me. If you have to kiss, keep it short and sweet. This isn't Amsterdam.

5) **And No Nudity**. No, I've never had someone get completely naked in my office but it's just a matter of time. I've had women strip down to their underwear and I've had men take off their shirts. The problem is there's absolutely nothing sexy about doing this in an office. It's just weird and uncomfortable. So don't do it. If you want to show off your body, wear form-fitting clothes.

6) **No Special Effects**. It only happened once but I'll never forget it. Two actors performed a scene where one of them is tied up in a chair and the other is interrogating him. Halfway through the scene, the second guy hauls off and slaps his partner across the face. I guess the actor in the chair had a blood capsule hidden in his mouth. His intention was to bite down and have blood trickle down his chin. But that's not what happened. He snapped his head too hard and blood sprayed out of his mouth, splattering all over our nice white walls. There was a moment of silence, then the owner of the agency started screaming. I forget the rest.

Of course, all the rules from the last chapter apply here. Keep it under five minutes, choose something contemporary, and be sure to pick a role that you would be cast in.

"Do scenes in your office ever go well?"

Over the years, I've signed many people based on scenes done in my office. A good actor will shine under any circumstances. True talent can never be denied.

So don't worry about the setting. Agents are really good at spotting the seeds of talent that can excite us enough to represent someone.

End Game

I usually signal the end of a meeting by asking an actor if they have any questions about the company or me. At this point, actors always waste their last chance to make an impression by asking the same boring questions.

A common one is *"How many clients do you have?"* This question comes up like clockwork. And I always think, what do you care? Does it really matter? If I say 150 instead of 100, are you going to turn me down if I offer to represent you?

Granted, there are some low level agencies that make a living by signing hundreds of clients in the hope that someone hits. It's called "the spaghetti theory". Just toss everyone against the wall and see who sticks.

A little bit of homework should weed those people out quickly. Check with SAG. If you're a member, they'll tell you how many actors are signed with an agency. And if you're not a member, I'm sure by now you know someone who is.

The next mindless question is, *"Do you have a lot of people like me?"* The answer is simple. Of course not! Why do you think you're here???

This brings up "conflicts" again. Agents often tell actors they're not interested because they have too many people like them on their list. Sometimes this is a line; sometimes it's not.

Agents break up their client lists by types. These categories are usually based on age, race and looks. So if you're a 40 year old character actor and I already have 6 clients in that category, then sorry — you're a conflict. There's no way I can sign you because even if you're good, I don't really need you.

The big exception to this rule is beautiful young people. If you're 21 and gorgeous, the world is yours. I can never have enough of these actors because they're in a very marketable category.

On the other hand, if you're a heavyset Eskimo, the odds are I'm only going to need one.

Here's an example of a real conflict. I once represented a successful black actor in his twenties. Let's call him Wayne. Wayne was generating a great deal of money for the company and he was a top priority to all the agents.

One day, I was presented with the opportunity to sign an actor who was an up and coming version of Wayne. I was sure we could represent them both equally well but I decided to treat my client with the respect that he deserved.

What did I do? I told Wayne everything and then I asked him how he felt. After giving it some thought, he told me flat out that he was uncomfortable with the idea.

So I passed on the actor. And I didn't give it a second thought.

The bottom line is that conflicts can be very real but if you're already in my office, there's probably no need to worry.

Besides, as clients move up the food chain and start booking more substantial work, there will be roles that they'll no longer audition for because they've outgrown them. When this happens, I'm going to need people to fill that opening.

A Word About Pocket Clients

There have been times when I've been the only agent in the office who wants to sign an actor. When this happens, I have two possible choices.

The first is to go along with the others and pass. There's no point in signing an actor if everyone isn't interested. It's just a waste of time and I'm going to end up doing all the work.

The other choice is to take the actor on as a "pocket client". This means that I will unofficially represent the actor and none of the other agents will have to work for him.

The downside to this type of deal is that you're not actually signed with the company and the agent who pockets you will always give the real clients top priority.

But if you should happen to book a job or two, it might help spark the interest of the other agents. This usually leads to a second chance at becoming a signed client.

What If The Answer Is No?

John McEnroe was a great tennis player. He was also a poor loser. When McEnroe lost a match, he would throw his racquet down and curse at the judges. There's no doubt about it, he was a unique character but I wouldn't suggest using him as a role model.

If an agent passes on you, it's important that you handle it well. Getting angry serves no purpose. Why burn a bridge that you may need to cross in the future?

I once had an actor go off on me after I passed. He said I was making a big mistake and that I would be sorry when he made it big.

Two years later, I was working at a different company and one of the agents brought the same guy in for a meeting. Needless to say, I made sure that we didn't sign him.

And you know what? The actor hadn't booked a single job in all that time. I wonder why.

So be smart about rejection. If an agent passes on you, ask for feedback. You need to know why you weren't signed. Maybe there's something you can work on before you take any more meetings.

It's also important to maintain the relationship. The agent must've liked something about you or he wouldn't have brought you in to meet. That makes him an ally. So stay in touch about any developments in your career.

You never know. Sometimes, the wheel comes full circle and you might get another shot.

What If The Answer Is Yes?

Looks like all your hard work paid off. Good for you. Now you're probably wondering what happens next.

The first thing you have to do is sign a contract. The agreement is good for 1 year with an option to renew for up to 3 more years. Naturally, both parties have to agree before the contract can be renewed.

Here's the inside story on agency contracts. A year may seem like a long time but you have an out that's built into the agreement. If you don't work at least ten days during any ninety-day period, you have the right to walk away. This is for your own protection.

You will also be asked to sign a check authorization. This is a legal document that allows your agent to accept payment on your behalf.

Here's how it works. When you book an acting job, the production company will send your money to the agent. He will deduct a 10% commission, then forward the rest to you.

This is standard operating procedure. It allows us to keep track of your earnings. It also insures that we won't have to take legal action if you refuse to pay your commissions.

Once all the papers are signed, you should give your new agent about a hundred headshots. Your resume will be stored on the company's computer so that changes can be made quickly. And if you have a reel, you should give your agent at least five copies.

And that's it. You're good to go.

When an agent offers to sign you, it's time to go out and celebrate. Your career has taken a big leap forward and you've earned the right to party.

Then, after you sober up, get ready for a whole new set of problems. The next chapter deals with all the little things that can go wrong once you actually become someone's client.

Final Thoughts

When meeting with an actor seeking representation, it's easy for an agent to say no. "No" requires zero effort. No. That's it. End of meeting. You walk out of my office and out of my life. You are now someone else's problem.

On the other hand, "yes" involves a huge amount of work. Yes means that I'm going to be committing lots of time and energy into getting your career off the ground. And it's not just about me. The other agents in the office are going to have to work hard too.

Another consideration is the expense. Signing a client costs money. All those submissions, phone calls and script copies add up.

Signing a new client means a professional and financial commitment on the part of the agent and the agency. We tend to take this very seriously.

So don't give us a reason to say no. Because if you do, we will. It's that simple.

How to be a Good Client

"All the people throughout my life who were naysayers pissed me off. But they've all given me a fervor, an angry ambition that cannot be stopped - and I look forward to finding a therapist and working on that."

— Tobey Maguire

How to Be a Good Client 6

So you finally got an agent. Good for you. That means you get to kick back and wait for the auditions to start pouring in. After all, you've worked hard to get to this point. Now it's time to chill by the pool and let someone else do the work. Right?

Wrong.

Getting signed by an agent is a great accomplishment. But now that you've gotten to this point, it's essential that you continue to make all the right moves. Your behavior as a client will greatly affect your chances for success.

So take a few days off and celebrate. Work on your Oscar speech. Practice signing autographs. And when you're done dreaming, it's time to get back to work.

Make Yourself Stand Out

Keep in mind that you're not the only client at the agency. Your agent is probably working for over a hundred actors and they've all been there a lot longer than you. So you need to stand out. You need to become more than a name on a list.

First, you have to build a relationship with your new agent. There are many ways to do this. Here's a suggestion that when done properly, has always worked on me.

Invite your agent to lunch.

This gives you both an hour to get to know each other without any interruptions. By doing this, you've created a great opportunity to make an impression as a real human being, not just as a needy actor.

The key to making lunch a success is — don't talk about acting. If you start complaining about how you're not getting enough auditions, the agent will go back to the office with a bad taste in his mouth. And that's not what you want.

Instead, try having a normal conversation, just like you would with a friend. See if you can find some common ground. Talk about your favorite movies or the price of tea in China. The topic doesn't really matter. The idea here is to make a connection.

If you can pull this off, then you're halfway home to establishing a solid working relationship with your agent.

I can already hear some of you whining — "Do I really have to spend money on my agent?" Sure, why not? It's called a business expense. Get over it. I take casting directors out to lunch all the time.

And besides, you don't have to spend a fortune. I would never expect a new client to take me to the latest hot spot in Beverly Hills. A nice juicy burger at some joint around the corner will do just fine.

Speaking of food, I used to represent an established actor who would come by once a month with a breakfast tray loaded with bagels and all kinds of spreads. We never knew when he was coming but when we least expected it, there he was — with a smile on his face and a tray full of goodies.

This was definitely above and beyond the call of duty but it was his way of saying thanks for all our hard work. I can't begin to tell you how much good will this generated. And when casting directors didn't want to see him, we would try just a little bit harder to get him in the door.

"What else has a client done to make themselves stand out?"

My client Jimmy is married to an attractive lady who happens to be a lounge singer. One night, he invited me to watch her perform. The show was fantastic and afterwards, the three of us hung out for an hour and had a few drinks.

By spending time with his wife, I got to know Jimmy in a different way. I learned that he was much more than an actor. He was also a man whose life revolved around a very special lady.

Another client named Mary liked to work at those creepy Renaissance Fairs. I always thought that whole scene was a little weird and I told her so.

Then one day, she dropped by my office in full costume with several pictures of herself in character. This led to a great chat about that strange world and this actress quickly became much more than a name on my list.

"So she just dropped by without an appointment? I've always been told not to do that."

It all depends on your expectations. I don't have all day to chat with clients. My job is to work the phones and get auditions. But if you catch me at the right time, we might be able to sit down and talk for a few minutes.

Naturally, it helps if you have a good reason for coming in. Let's say you need to pick up a script. Or maybe we're running low on pictures. Those are both good excuses to pop in and see your agent.

If it's really busy, you'll probably just get a quick hello. But you know what? That's a good thing too. Just seeing you in the office makes an impression. And that's better than nothing.

I would also suggest that you try to look different every time you visit your agent. That means changing your appearance.

I used to work with an actor who had a real rock and roll style. Long hair, torn jeans, the whole look. Then he popped in one day wearing a business suit.

At first, I didn't even recognize him. The other agents were shocked too. His hair was combed back into a ponytail and he looked like, well, an agent.

This guy knew exactly what he was doing. He was aware that people saw him as a rocker so he went the extra mile to show us that he could play different kinds of parts.

These are all good examples of ways that clients have made an impression on me. There are many, many others. Be creative and think up some new ones.

"What's the worst impression a client has ever made on you?"

I guess the worst impression is to make no impression. Believe it or not, I once spent five minutes hitting on a woman at a Christmas party before I realized that she was my client.

Was I embarrassed? Of course not. I have 120 clients and she has 3 agents. Why hadn't she made it her job to get to know the people who are responsible for her career?

It doesn't happen often but every now and then, I'll sign an actor and a few months later, I'll realize that I haven't seen them since we first started working together. They'll go out on auditions, we'll talk on the phone, but there's no real physical contact. As a result, they're complete strangers to me, nothing more than a name on my list.

So it really doesn't matter what you do or how you do it. The goal here is to create a chance for your agent to become familiar with you as an individual. If you can accomplish this, then you're already halfway home.

Behave Like A Professional

The early stages of our relationship are very important. You don't want to create any problems. That means learning how to behave like a professional.

The first step is to accept that you are indeed a professional. This is a business and you're an actor who is about to meet all those casting directors that never came to your showcase. Your behavior will reflect on both you and your agent.

So you have to be on your game. That means being prepared. Like a Navy Seal, you have to be 100% ready to deliver the goods in any setting.

If you get an audition for a big movie, it's your responsibility to do some homework on the director. Look up his credits on The Internet Movie Database (*www.imdb.com*). Know his background. This could come in handy if the casting director engages you in a conversation about the project.

The same thing applies to television. If I get you an audition for a TV show, you damn well better not tell me that you've never seen the program. The casting director is going to expect you to be familiar with the show's style of acting.

If it's a sitcom, you'll need to know if the comedy is broad or realistic. The same thing goes for drama. "The West Wing" has a quick rhythm whereas "NYPD Blue" is much more natural.

Here's a great idea. Create your own personal library by taping an episode of every single TV show that's on the air. Then, when you get an audition, you can dig out the tape and watch it.

Studying TV shows is one of the many things you can do while you're waiting for the phone to ring.

"Got it. What else can I do to be a professional?"

I've said it before and I'll say it again — don't lie! Trust me, you will always get caught.

Case in point. A big studio feature was recently looking to cast an actor in his late thirties from New England. The part required horseback riding ability because there would be a scene where he would have to race against the lead.

My client Peter is 38, grew up in Vermont and has "horseback riding" listed under the Special Skills section of his resume. Perfect, right? Yeah, I thought so too.

So I got Peter a meeting with the casting director who liked his reading and sent him to meet Chuck, the guy in charge of the horses. He would have to take a fairly basic riding test at Chuck's ranch.

Remember Jack Palance in "City Slickers"? That's exactly what Chuck looked like. He turned out to be a retired stuntman who had grown up in the business and didn't take crap from anyone.

So anyway, Peter goes to the ranch, climbs up on the horse, and after 10 seconds, Chuck tells him to get the hell off and never come back.

It turned out that my client had exaggerated a little about his level of expertise with horses.

The casting director was ticked off that I had wasted her time and she really let me have it. Rest assured that I passed it all on in kind to my idiot client.

That's why you should never lie to your agent. You have nothing to gain and everything to lose.

One of my other pet peeves is lateness. I have absolutely no tolerance for actors who are always running late for auditions. This kind of behavior makes me go ballistic.

Besides being unprofessional, not showing up on time tends to throw off a casting director's schedule. It creates a negative energy in the room that doesn't help when you finally start to audition. Why make life any harder than it needs to be?

If you have a 4:00 audition, you should plan on being there by 3:30. That gives you time to relax, hit the bathroom and go over your lines one last time.

And yes, I understand that sometimes it's not your fault. It's easy to get stuck in unexpected traffic. When this happens, call me on your cell so I can let casting know that you're running late.

All those years I worked in production taught me how crucial it is to always be on time. I expect my clients to feel the same way.

Being a professional also means being reachable at all times. You would think this one is a no-brainer but it shocks me how many actors make this mistake. Some of you are very skilled at dropping off the face of the planet. Don't you want your agent to call you? Isn't that the whole point?

Recently, I signed a young actor who wanted to work on a soap. This was a realistic goal because he definitely had the looks for it.

The first day after I signed him, I heard that "General Hospital" needed to see some actors right away for a last minute part. They only had time to read a few people and the casting director agreed to give my new client a shot.

Perfect timing, right? The only problem was that I couldn't reach the guy. I left countless messages but he never returned any of them. The whole day went by and the opportunity was wasted.

The next day, he finally showed up at my office with tears in his eyes. The knucklehead had spent the entire day on the beach and never bothered to check his messages. He figured nothing would happen on our first day of working together.

The lesson here is to get a cell phone. And don't tell me you can't afford it. There are plenty of great deals out there. So go buy one and then keep it with you at all times.

You should also have a reliable answering machine at home. Play it safe and check in every few hours.

An agent expects his call to be returned as quickly as possible. This is one of the golden rules.

And don't forget to let your agent know if you're leaving town. I don't care if it's a day trip or a week in Hawaii. We need to know that you're not going to be around. So book out as soon as possible.

There's nothing worse than calling your client with a great appointment and having them return your call from a pay phone in Turkey. (Yes, this actually happened!)

"What about my headshots? Will I need to get new ones when I sign with an agent?"

If you followed my advice in Chapter 2, your headshot should be perfect and ready to go. But yes, there is a chance that your agent might want new pictures. And that's fine. After all, now it's his turn to use your headshot as a marketing tool and he has to be confident that it will get the job done.

I would say that most agents ask 1 out of every 4 new clients to take new pictures. If you end up being the lucky 1, find out why your agent doesn't like your current shots so that you can address those concerns with your photographer.

This brings up another important issue. Please make sure that I always have enough pictures in the office. I hate it when a casting director requests your headshot and my assistant tells me we're fresh out.

Professional actors always have 50 extra headshots at home. This way, when my assistant calls to inform you that we're out, you can rush some pictures over right away. This beats waiting five days for the lab to print your order.

"Anything else?"

I mentioned earlier that agents are judged by who they represent. This is why you have to behave like a professional. Everything you do reflects on us.

To illustrate this point, I'm going to close this section with two worst case scenarios that happened to other agents. In both stories, the actors in question were dropped as clients.

HORRIBLE STORY #1

An actor named Mark was up for the lead in a network pilot. He had already auditioned twice and the feedback was excellent

On a Friday afternoon, the casting director called his agent to say there would be one final audition on Monday. If that went well, Mark would get a chance to test at the network.

Sounds like a plan, right?

Unfortunately, Mark made one little decision over the weekend that in retrospect probably wasn't very smart.

He had his tongue pierced.

Mark always wanted to do it and he honestly felt it was right for the character. The problem was that he showed up on Monday with his tongue swollen to twice its size. The guy could barely get the words out.

The casting director freaked out. It was his role to lose and that's exactly what Mark did.

HORRIBLE STORY #2

An established director named Jeffrey Newbauer is busy preparing to shoot his next movie. He's working extremely long days and is on the verge of exhaustion.

Now picture this. It's Sunday morning and he's in bed, sound asleep. The phone rings...

<u>Director</u>:	Hello?
<u>Voice</u>:	Is this Jeffrey Newbauer, the film director?
<u>Director</u>:	Yeah. Who's this?
<u>Voice</u>:	My name's Peter Smith. I auditioned for you on Friday.
<u>Director</u>:	You're who?
<u>Voice</u>:	Oh c'mon, you remember. I used a gold lighter.
<u>Director</u>:	What do you want?
<u>Voice</u>:	I'm just wondering. Have you made any decisions yet?
<u>Director</u>:	Click.
<u>Voice</u>:	Hello? Hello?

I swear this story is true. The actor tracked down the director's number and really believed he was being proactive. Sadly, no one else saw it that way.

His actions set off a series of ugly phone calls that ended with his agent telling him to look for new representation.

Don't Have Unreasonable Expectations

Actors often forget that their agents have a life outside the office.

Trust me — most of us are not robots sent back in time to make your life miserable. Agents are just like normal people. We have families and friends and other interests that occupy our time when we're not busy slaving away at the office.

So unless you're generating a huge amount of money as an actor, you shouldn't expect your agent to be available to you every single day of the year.

Let me explain what I mean. A client named Brian once called to invite me to a screening of a short film he had done before I signed him. It sounded like fun and I agreed to go.

Then I found out the screening was being held on a Saturday morning at ten! I couldn't believe it. Weekends fall under "personal time" and I was stunned that he actually expected me to show up.

So I told him to forget it. There was no way I was going. Brian was disappointed but promised to lend me his VHS copy. The moment he said that, I realized Brian didn't care about anyone except himself.

Think about it. We're talking about a twenty minute movie here and it's not like this screening was the only opportunity for me to see it. After all, he had a copy on tape the whole time. There was no reason to drag my butt out of bed on a Saturday morning when

I could watch the damn thing in the comfort of my own home.

This kind of behavior is selfish. I would've respected the actor much more if he had told me about the screening and then offered to get me a tape so I wouldn't have to show up on a Saturday.

But what Brian did is nothing compared to the actions of a very well known actor named Jason.

Since he was a big money maker, Jason had home numbers on all his agents. This is standard practice for important clients. Most actors know not to abuse this trust but this particular guy didn't understand professional boundaries.

Here's what happened. Jason was having Sunday brunch with some industry friends who gave him a lead on a new film. Eager to get this information to his agents, Jason picked up the phone and called the owner of the company at home.

Unfortunately, the owner's mother had just passed away and he was busy making funeral plans.

At this point, any other human being would have apologized and gotten off the line as quickly as possible. But not Jason. He actually had the nerve to ask who would be looking out for his career while the owner was taking time off from work.

My boss dropped him on the spot. Then he called yours truly on Monday morning and ordered me to throw out all of Jason's pictures, resumes and demo reels.

This is what I mean when I say — don't have unreasonable expectations. These incidents tend to mark you in the eyes of your agents. And who needs that kind of negativity?

Never Let Your Personal Life Get In The Way

I have a client named Shannon who constantly gets stuck playing the character who gives all the exposition in a scene. She's always the doctor who has to explain an illness or the cop who has to fill in the hero about a crime scene.

Shannon was getting bored with these parts so I pulled a favor and got her an audition for a great role that was central to the plot of a "JAG" episode. The entire episode was about her character and there were some really meaty scenes.

Naturally, Shannon was thrilled at the opportunity but guess what? She never made it to the appointment. It turned out that the night before, she had a big fight with her boyfriend and wasn't in the right state of mind to audition.

This is the kind of thing that makes me want to rip my hair out. Who cares about her stupid love life? Auditioning is a huge part of every actor's job and personal problems should never get in the way.

Can you imagine what would happen if I told a client that I hadn't been able to get them an audition because I was bummed about an argument with my girlfriend?

The client would fire me in a New York minute and I wouldn't blame them one bit.

So remember, professionals never allow their personal life to intrude on their work. And if you have problems that won't go away, take some time off and deal with them. You're better off doing that than alienating your agents.

Learn The System

Now that you have representation, it's important that you understand how agents divide their duties. This knowledge will help you navigate your way through our system much more effectively.

The first thing you need to know is that agents don't split up the client list. (That only happens at huge places like CAA and William Morris.) When you sign with a company that has more than one agent, all the agents end up representing you together.

The person who brought you in for the initial meeting becomes your point person. This agent stands to make more money since he is responsible for you being a client. The two of you will probably bond right away because you share an immediate connection.

But it would be a mistake not to get to know everyone else too. You have to connect with all the agents, not just your point person.

Like all salesmen, agents are assigned territories. We break the town up by casting directors. Different agents cover different casting directors. This is how we divide responsibilities.

That's why it's crucial that you get to know everyone. Think about it. If the company has three agents and one of them doesn't really know you, then you're going to miss out on a third of the town.

I once signed a great actress named Alice who had just graduated from Julliard. She had done some serious dramatic work in school but there was nothing on her resume (or in her personality) to indicate that she could be funny.

One of the other agents in my office didn't agree. The two of them had really connected and she felt that Alice could book a sitcom. So she set up an audition for a role on "Everybody Loves Raymond" and sure enough, Alice got the job.

What can I say? Sometimes, I'm wrong. (But I signed her, so I still win!)

Granted, it's hard to click with everyone but you still have to make the effort. And don't worry. Once you start booking work, all the agents will be racing to get you out there. At that point, life will become much easier.

Make Nice With The Assistant

Everything I said earlier about assistants goes double here. Now that you're a signed client, these people are your lifeline to the agents. They can be your best friends or your worst enemies. I would suggest going with the first.

My assistant always fills me in on client behavior — good and bad. If it took him all day to reach you, I'm going to hear about it. By the same token, if you always go out of your way to make his life easier, I'm going to hear about that too.

Assistants are like field agents in the outer office that report back to headquarters.

Don't Forget About Christmas

I love the holidays! There are a million parties to attend, everyone's in a great mood, and gifts are constantly pouring into the office.

So don't forget to give your agents a little something. It doesn't have to be expensive. A bottle of wine is always nice. Just make sure you send something.

Now don't get me wrong. I'm not a greedy guy. At least, not during the holidays. It's just that we work hard and Christmas gifts are a great way of expressing your gratitude.

Besides, we keep a list of every present so that we can send a thank you note in January. Wouldn't it be kind of weird if your name wasn't on that list?

Always Listen To Your Agent

When your career takes off, life will get a lot more complicated. Key decisions will have to be made and what you say no to will become just as important as what you say yes to.

At times like this, you have to listen carefully to what your agent tells you. It's important that you have enough information to make an intelligent choice.

That doesn't mean you have to agree with everything an agent says but you should still listen carefully to what's being said. It's hard to be objective about yourself. Your agent might be able to spot problems that you would never notice.

I always give a great deal of thought to every crucial career decision. Sometimes clients take my advice, sometimes they don't. I have no problem with that as long as I feel that I've been heard. The final choice will always belong to the actor.

After all, it's your career. Not mine.

When I first became an agent, I represented a young actress named Deena. She had worked in a few successful independent films and was looking forward to her next project.

One day, a great script came across my desk for a very low budget movie. All the leads were male but there were some good supporting roles for women.

Luckily, the casting director was an old friend who trusted my instincts. She agreed to bring Deena in right away to meet the director and producers.

Then I learned that the auditions were being held at the director's apartment. This didn't sound right. Deena is a very attractive girl and I was more than a little concerned.

The casting director assured me that she would be there too and that everything was on the up and up. I still had some reservations but I really loved that script.

So I advised her to go and meet these guys. Some of her actor friends told her she was nuts. Deena chose to trust me. And sure enough, there were no problems and she ended up getting the part.

The movie was "Swingers".

Deena was cast as one of the women that Vince Vaughn and Jon Favreau hook up with during their trip to Vegas. Needless to say, she had no regrets about listening to her agent.

Keep Going The Extra Mile

Finally, you have to continue doing all the things you were doing while you were still searching for an agent. If anything, this is the time to double your efforts.

So whatever you do, don't stop studying. Keep flexing your acting muscles. And since you're going to be auditioning a lot more now, this might be the time to switch from scene study to a cold reading workshop.

If you think you don't need to stay in class, consider this. After starring in "The Cider House Rules" and "Wonder Boys", Tobey Maguire decided to take a break and go back to acting school. I think that says a lot about his dedication to the craft of acting and you should learn from his example.

Going the extra mile also means being completely prepared for every single audition.

I used to represent a very successful British actor who would lock himself away in a rented studio before every audition. He would spend an entire hour in there, practicing his lines with no interruptions. This guy had one of the best booking ratios I've ever seen.

You should also continue to pursue stage work and you should even consider performing in more showcases. Since you already have representation, you can now focus exclusively on inviting casting directors. Hell, I might even be able to help.

This reminds me of a client named Jon. He was a nice kid who always said the wrong thing.

One day, he called to invite me to a play that he was in. This is exactly what he said:

"This show I'm doing is really, really bad but I have a great scene in the second act. I hope you can come."

I told Jon that if I pitched him the way he just pitched his play, he would never work again.

Final Thoughts

Being an agent is a tough job. So please don't make our life any tougher. There are only so many minutes in the day. Learn to respect that.

The time will come when you will need me to fight for you. I have found that it's easier to win these battles if I genuinely believe in the cause.

So let's recap:

1) Make Yourself Stand Out
2) Behave Like A Professional
3) Never Let Your Personal Life Get In The Way
4) Learn The System
5) Make Nice With The Assistant
6) Don't Forget About Christmas
7) Always Listen To Your Agent
8) Keep Going The Extra Mile

Following this advice will help you maintain a healthy relationship with your agent. And if you can pull that off, you'll be light years ahead of all the other clients on his list.

Pilot
Season

"Fame is a very unnatural condition. When you stop to realize that Abraham Lincoln was probably never seen by more than 400 people in a single evening, and that I used to enter over 40 million homes every week due to the power of television, you have to admit the situation is not normal."

— Chevy Chase

Pilot Season 7

Back in New York, I had a lot of close friends who were struggling actor types. They were all very creative people and I always enjoyed spending time with them.

Over the years, I started to notice a strange migration pattern among their kind.

As soon as the holidays were over, my friends would pack their bags and head out to LA for something called "pilot season". Then three months later, they would all come back, looking like they'd been through hell.

Now that I'm a talent agent, I wish I could travel back in time and save them from this foolish behavior.

For some strange reason, actors believe that during pilot season, agents and casting directors will become more receptive to the hordes of unknowns with stars in their eyes.

Nothing could be further from the truth.

Going through pilot season without an agent is like trying to survive a war without a gun. And even with representation, there's no guarantee you're going to get seen by all the stressed out casting directors who are buried under a pile of work and impossible deadlines.

So let's talk about pilot season and hopefully, I'll be able to shed some light on this mysterious but exciting time of year.

What Is Pilot Season?

Pilot season starts in the middle of January and lasts till the end of April. During this period, over one hundred television pilots are produced, with each show hoping to land a slot on the new fall schedule.

When pilot season comes to an end, the networks pick their favorites and turn them into a series. The ones that aren't chosen vanish from sight, never to be seen by the American public.

In 2004, there were 128 pilots produced at a cost of over one hundred millions dollars.

Less than 40 made it on the air.

That's why pilot season is one big roll of the dice. Even if you get lucky and book a pilot, there's no guarantee it will get picked up as a series.

The thing to remember is that every pilot has a set number of series regular roles, meaning characters that will appear in every episode. These parts are the holy grail of the agency business.

If you land a series regular role on the right pilot and it gets turned into a hit show, you just became an incredibly wealthy individual. I would suggest that you start looking for a really good accountant.

Before he became famous, George Clooney was the king of pilot season. Year after year, he would always book great pilots but none of them ever got picked up. I never met the guy but I would imagine he was getting pretty frustrated with the whole process.

Then one warm winter day, George booked a role on yet another pilot. This one was set in a hospital's emergency room. The rest is history.

That's why when pilot season hits, there's a mad scramble by every agent in town to get their clients auditions for all these new pilots that might become the next "ER".

Pilot season is the time of year when you will always find agents working long hours and taking loads of scripts home for weekend reading. The volume of work is overwhelming and the competition is fierce. An agency's future can be made or destroyed by how many pilots they book.

It's a stressful process and after working as an agent for over ten years, I have finally discovered one of the biggest secrets in Hollywood:

Pilot season is stupid.

I'm serious. From a financial point of view, it doesn't make any sense. Millions of dollars are spent every year to produce these pilots and most of them never get seen by anyone except the network suits.

So why do it? Why waste so much money? I think the answer is obvious. No one has been able to figure out a better way.

Since network executives are unable (or unwilling) to make decisions about new shows without actually seeing a pilot episode, this insane practice will continue until someone finds a more efficient and less costly system.

"Is pilot season the only time pilots are made?"

In the last few years, more and more pilots have gone into production during the fall, right before the holidays. The reason for this is that studios want to get a jump on signing good talent before pilot season begins.

In the old days, there were only a handful of networks opposing each other. But now, thanks to the success of cable, there's much more competition.

I remember when the FOX Network first came on the air to compete with CBS, NBC, and ABC. Everyone laughed and said they were crazy.

But FOX had the last laugh. By fighting back with strong programming, they were able to attract a fair share of the marketplace. Viewers started to tune in every week for shows like "The Simpsons" and "Beverly Hills, 90210".

Now, the TV landscape is a brand new world. In addition to UPN and the WB Network, there are several cable companies producing very successful original programming.

Here's a partial list:

HBO	Showtime	Lifetime
Bravo	Comedy Central	MTV
USA	Nickelodeon	Animal Planet
F/X	Sci-Fi Channel	Disney Channel

This is great news. All these new stations mean more work for everyone. And a lot more series regular roles that need to be cast.

The Name Game

A good friend at CBS once told me that TV shows are just filler between commercials.

That's why most of the series regular roles on pilots end up going to major name actors. The presence of a star doesn't guarantee success but it sure helps sell the show to the advertisers.

Back in the day, an unknown model like Ted Danson could walk in and book the lead on "Cheers". If they were shooting that pilot today, the outcome would be very different.

With few exceptions, most of the programs currently on the air have at least one star to anchor the show. The ones that don't, have recognizable faces known to every network and studio in town.

Even shows like "Smallville" which feature fresh young faces have a guy like John Schneider playing Clark's dad. The same goes for "The O.C." and "Seventh Heaven".

The bad news is that this obsession with name talent is only going to get worse. Thanks to the success of reality television, there are now less time slots available during prime time for conventional programming.

And no, reality television is not a passing fad. These shows cost very little to produce and they generate substantial revenue for the networks. This kind of success means that "Survivor" and "American Idol" are here to stay.

So as the competition increases to get new shows on the air, name actors will continue to be the best way for producers to hedge their bets.

The good news is that there will always be other series regular roles besides the leads. David Caruso may be in charge over at "CSI: Miami" but he's got a team of investigators who are always there to back him up.

And each one of those actors is making a mint.

"So you think it's still possible for an unknown like me to book a series regular role?"

It's definitely possible but it sure as hell isn't easy.

To help you understand pilot season, I'm going to take an imaginary client through the entire process — from start to finish.

Let's call the client "Lisa". She's 24, pretty, and great with comedy. Lisa doesn't have a strong resume but after watching her perform in an improv show, I took a chance and signed her.

Lisa also thinks her agent is very handsome but that has nothing to do with this discussion.

The Casting Process

After the holidays, agents are faced with about two weeks of dead time. Then suddenly, right around the third week of January, breakdowns start appearing for pilots.

The one hour dramas usually come out first because those pilots take longer to produce than the average sitcom. They have to allow time for postproduction which includes sound editing, special effects and music.

Half-hours comedies, on the other hand, appear throughout the entire season. Most of them are shot in front of a live audience and this cuts down on postproduction time.

Either way, every pilot has to be completely finished by the beginning of May. I'll explain why later.

Since my client Lisa is new, I'm going to focus on her strengths. I signed her because she's funny so my plan is to target all my casting friends who are working on half hour pilots. My pitch will be that she's a bright new talent who's waiting to be discovered.

(Yes, lines like that actually work, especially when you say them really fast.)

The first rule of pilot season is that no one knows what they want. Remember, pilots are just prototypes for a series so nothing is written in stone. Producers will make any changes necessary to give their shows a better shot at getting picked up by the network.

As casting begins, I've seen series regular roles change race, age and in some cases, even sex. The character descriptions on the breakdown tend to get dated very quickly.

A great example of how characters evolve during pilot season is the David Kelly show "Snoops" which aired back in 1999. The lead was the beautiful Gina Gershon who played one of several female private investigators.

Guess what? When they first started casting, all those characters were male.

That's why agents have to stay current with casting directors. I may get told that a certain character is Hispanic but who knows? If I call back in a few days, they might've changed it to Asian.

Needless to say, lazy agents don't do very well during pilot season.

So, keeping all that in mind, I'm going to send Lisa out for every part I think she can play, despite the initial character description. I feel confident doing this because I've already seen her perform a wide variety of roles in her sketch show.

I will also encourage her not to judge the quality of every pilot. It's tough to tell what the finished product is going to be like, especially without the actors. The right cast can really bring a script to life.

For the record, I'm the guy who read the pilot script for "Friends" and thought it was boring.

"Do actors have to prepare differently for a pilot audition?"

You should always give your all but pilots are a little bit different.

First, it's crucial that you read the entire script. Sides are not enough. You have to understand how your character fits into the total picture.

Reading the script will also help you appreciate the tone of the project. If it's a comedy, you need to know if the humor is over the top like "Malcolm in the Middle" or if it's more grounded like "Scrubs". That will help you make strong choices for the audition.

Nothing upsets me more than when I go to the trouble of copying a script for a client and they don't even bother to pick it up. That kind of behavior is inexcusable.

Besides, what if the casting director asks you a question about the story? What are you going to say?

Next, you need to understand that the creators of these pilots aren't always sure what they want. They're looking for someone to come in and show them.

Auditioning for pilots gives you an opportunity to create a character from top to bottom. If the show gets picked up, viewers are going to be watching it for many years. That means the characters have to be memorable.

On the show "Seinfeld", no one wrote the character of Kramer. The words may have been on paper but Michael Richards is the one who went in there and gave him life.

I once had a client who auditioned for a series regular role on a UPN comedy that was poorly written. None of the characters were especially memorable and the producers were very concerned.

My client made a strong choice and played his role in a deadpan monotone. No one else had thought to do this. And it worked! Suddenly, the character was incredibly unique and he ended up booking the job.

So work hard and bring something to the part that isn't on the page. You have to make it your own. That's the way to book a series regular role.

Callbacks

In the world of pilots, one callback is never enough. There's too much at stake. Producers usually want to see actors a few times, especially if the script is undergoing a lot of changes.

Sometimes you will be called in to a mix and match session, meaning you get to audition with actors who are up for the other parts on the show. This helps the producers get a sense of the entire cast.

If a star is attached to the project, you might also be asked to read with him. This is great news because reading with a celebrity usually elevates the quality of your work. The trick is not to be intimidated. Actors who get nervous around celebrities never get asked to work with them.

Speaking of nervousness, it's imperative that you come across as confident. The producers have to believe they can trust you to get the job done.

It doesn't matter if you give a great audition. If you look nervous, they're not going to give you the part. There's too much money at stake to hire someone who might crack under the grind of a weekly production schedule.

Remember when I said it's important to be likeable? That goes double during pilot season. Producers know that if their show gets picked up, they're going to be spending a lot of time with the cast. So it definitely helps if they like you from the start.

Now let's get back to Lisa. She's been auditioning for a lot of pilots and the feedback has been good. That's a great sign. Now I just have to find the right part.

That's why agents read every single pilot script that comes across their desk. It gives us a chance to picture our clients in the show.

After a few more breakdowns are released, it finally happens. I come across the perfect project for Lisa. It's a hilarious NBC pilot and the role is similar to one I saw her perform on stage. And bless the Gods, the casting director is a friend who has always trusted my taste.

So I make the call, Lisa auditions and bang! She gets her first callback.

I can hear Lisa's excitement over the phone when I tell her the good news. And you know what my one and only piece of advice is?

Don't make any changes.

I'm sure you're all familiar with the expression — "if it ain't broke, don't fix it". Well, that goes double during pilot season.

If the casting director decides to bring you back, that means you did something right. So when you meet the producers, it's very important that you read exactly the same way you did during the initial audition.

The same holds true for every single callback in the entire process. I don't care how many times the producers want to see you. Don't make changes.

Unfortunately, after a few callbacks, most inexperienced actors start to think, "They must be getting tired of seeing me read the same way. It's time to show them something completely different".

Bad move! The creators of these shows want continuity. They need to know you're talented enough to hit the same notes week after week if the show gets picked up.

Luckily, Lisa listens to me and gives them an exact copy of her original performance. She even wears the same outfit. They laugh hysterically and the casting director nods.

Lisa then gets two more callbacks, does a mix and match session, and even gets to read with Tony Danza who gives her a big hug after the audition.

Does this mean she booked the pilot? No, of course not. Life is never that easy. It just means that

Lisa is one of several women who are going to "test" for the part.

Did I forget to mention that actors have to go through a rigorous testing procedure if they want to book a series regular role on a pilot?

Testing At The Network

First, you have to understand that pilots are created by two separate entities — studios and networks.

The studios have deals with the networks and they're the ones who actually produce the pilot. When I say studios, I'm talking about companies like Universal, Imagine, and DreamWorks.

After all the pilots are shot, the networks pick the ones that are going to get turned into a series. They have the final say on every project that is produced during pilot season.

The studios and networks have a lot of money at stake during this process and they know that casting can easily make or break a show. This is why producers usually test 3 to 5 actors for each series regular role on a pilot.

"What exactly does 'testing' mean?"

It's just one more audition. The only difference is you'll be reading in a large room filled with tired executives who have forgotten how to express any human emotion.

These poor bastards have been testing actors every day since pilot season started. We're talking hundreds of actors for all the roles on every single pilot. As a result, they're unbelievably exhausted and very stressed out.

Remember all those laughs you got in the last four auditions? Forget it. That's over. Even if the executives love you, the odds are you'll never know it. They're simply too tired to laugh.

My clients have told me that testing is ten times harder than any other audition. The tension is overwhelming because there's so much riding on the outcome. Naturally, it's very hard to do your best work in this kind of environment.

I once knew a young actress who tested sixteen times during one pilot season and didn't book anything. The experience was so devastating that she quit the business and moved back home.

Now here's the bad news. Once is not enough. You have to test twice!

Testing for a series regular role is a two step process. First, you go to the studio for approval, and after that, you get to read at the network.

Sometimes, both tests are held in the same day. That works well because the studio acts as a warm-up for the network. Other times, the tests are scheduled for two separate days.

Sadly, the studio has the right to make cuts. This means if the executives don't think you're right for the part, they can stop you from testing at the network.

As an agent, it's hard to predict what the studio

will do. I've seen them approve everyone and I've also seen them pass on an entire group of actors.

Needless to say, it really stinks when you go through this extremely long process only to find yourself cut right before the finish line.

To complicate matters, actors are not allowed to test until a test deal is negotiated between their agent and the studio.

This is one of the most important documents in the life of an actor and merits its own section.

The Test Deal Agreement

This contract basically assumes that the actor testing is going to book the role, shoot the pilot and then work on the series for the next six years.

It covers every single deal point for both the pilot and the series, including payment, billing, dressing rooms, and a hundred other details.

Test deals are negotiated on behalf of every actor testing, even though everyone knows that only one of them is going to actually get the part.

You're probably thinking it would easier to wait until after the test, right? That way, we would only need to work on one deal and life would be much easier.

The problem there is the agent would have all the power. Once an offer is made, I know the network wants my client so I'm free to ask for anything I want. By locking the terms *before* the test, both parties are on a more equal playing field.

"What does the contract cover?"

In a word, everything.

The most important element in a test deal is the money. I have to negotiate how much my client will be paid for both the pilot and the possible series.

These figures are usually stated in terms like 40 and 20 or 30 and 15.

The first number is what an actor makes on the pilot. The second is what an actor will get paid per episode if the pilot is picked up.

In other words, 40 and 20 means $40,000 for the pilot and $20,000 for every episode of the show in the first season. That amount will be bumped up 5% every year the show remains on the air.

"Why is the pilot fee twice as much as the series money?"

Payment for the pilot is always more because the studio is paying for your exclusivity. That means you're not allowed to test for any other pilots because they need you to be available if their show gets picked up.

This period of exclusivity lasts till the end of June. By that time, the networks have made all their choices and have approved every series regular.

During this time, an actor is free to work on anything they want, except another pilot.

Sometimes, an actor who is in great demand will book a pilot and then another studio will allow him to test in "second position". This means they're betting the first pilot won't get picked up and then they'll be able to use the actor if theirs does.

That's a dangerous move because if both pilots go to series, the second show is completely screwed. They're going to have to spend a lot of money to recast the part and then re-shoot the entire pilot episode.

To avoid this kind of expense, very few actors are allowed to test in second position. Studios need exclusivity and that's why they pay so much for it.

"What else does the test deal cover?"

In addition to money, I have to determine my client's billing. If there are five series regulars on the show, I have to negotiate for the position in which the credit will appear during the main titles.

It's usually a given that star names will get the first and last card. Everything else is up for grabs.

I can't begin to tell you how many hours I've spent arguing whether my client should receive third or fourth position. It's always the little things that make a negotiation drag on for days.

Agents also have to bargain for the size and contents of the dressing room and trailer.

On a one hour series, actors are on location almost every single day, spending countless hours waiting in their trailers. It can get pretty claustrophobic in those things so I have to insure that my client is guaranteed an acceptable level of comfort and privacy.

Here's a list of all the basic trailers that are used on location:

Star Wagon
(holds 1 actor)

These trailers are large and spacious. They're usually assigned to the stars of the show.

Double Banger
(holds 2 actors)

Basically, this is a trailer that has been cut in half. Double Bangers are still fairly comfortable and roomy. The down side is you have a neighbor.

Triple Banger
(holds 3 actors)

This is a trailer that has been split into three compartments. At this size, the rooms are starting to get pretty small.

Honey Wagon
(holds 4 actors)

This is the bottom of the barrel. These trailers have been divided into four tiny spaces. It's like being in prison.

A newcomer like my client Lisa will probably end up in a Triple Banger but I'll fight like hell to get her a Double.

Now, let's talk about sitcoms.

On a half hour series, production usually takes place on a sound stage. Instead of a trailer, an actor is given a private dressing room which is essentially their home away from home.

As an agent, I can request that the contents of the dressing room be itemized in the agreement. Nothing is automatically a given but this list can include a private bathroom, phone, couch, refrigerator, and many other amenities.

Despite the type of show, I have to make sure that (except for star names) no one else gets a bigger dressing room or trailer than my client.

Equality becomes very important when a series runs for several years. If another actor has a TV in his dressing room and my client doesn't, I will definitely be hearing about it.

The deal also covers points like photo approval, merchandising, public appearances, and what kind of work an actor can and cannot accept while he is under contract.

Test deal agreements can be anywhere from five to twenty pages and they generally take several days to negotiate. An actor who is testing for a series regular role has to sign it before he is allowed to read at the network.

"So who negotiates the contract?"

In one corner, you have the brave agent, sword in hand, fighting valiantly to get the best possible deal for his client.

In the other, you have a fire-breathing lawyer who works in the business affairs department at the studio.

Every fight, I mean negotiation, begins the same way. The lawyer calls and introduces himself. Then, we chit chat for a few minutes. After that, he lays out the terms of the deal and makes me an offer.

Opening offers are always low, even insulting.

At this point, I always say that I need to think about it. Then, as soon as we hang up, I start to plan my counter offer. The figure will usually be very high to balance the studio's low opening.

This process goes on for several days until we finally settle on a number that is acceptable to both parties.

I usually have a good idea of where a deal is going to end up. If business affairs opens with $30,000 for the pilot and I counter at sixty, the odds are we're going to close somewhere in the forties.

The studio bases their first offer on many factors. The biggest one is an actor's quote. This refers to how much the actor received the last time he tested for a pilot.

Lawyers tend to give more weight to quotes if the actor actually booked the job. If one of my clients tested last year but didn't get it, the lawyer will argue that the quote has no value. Then I'll fight back by saying the numbers represent what the actor was worth at that time and there's no reason for me to accept less. If anything, I'd like to get a little bit more.

And round and round we'll go until the deal is closed.

In Lisa's case, she has no quote. This is her first test so it's my job to lock in some decent numbers. That way, if Lisa doesn't book the pilot, I'll have something to work with next time.

"But how do you negotiate a good deal when your client has almost no experience?"

When I have no ammo to fight with, the negotiation quickly becomes a war of attrition. I end up trying to wear the other side down. If they won't give me twenty, I ask for nineteen. No? How about eighteen five?

On occasion, I'll have another agent get on the phone and together, we'll play good cop/bad cop. A fresh voice can make a big difference.

Agents have to nickel and dime every point until we reach a deal that we can all live with. Then and only then, will we close and allow our clients to test.

"Have you ever had to play dirty to get what you want?"

During a negotiation, I try to conduct myself in a professional manner. Agents usually end up dealing with the same business affairs person several times during pilot season so there's no reason to piss anyone off.

That said, yes, sometimes we have to play dirty.

I was once stuck in the middle of a test deal that was going nowhere fast. It involved a young client who was relatively new and didn't have any quotes.

The business affairs person was a woman named Melinda. Every negotiation has some give and take but she wouldn't budge on one single point. Her argument was that since my client had no experience, she didn't deserve to be paid as much as the other actors who were testing.

I didn't buy that for a minute. After all, my client wouldn't be testing if the studio didn't think she was good enough to play the part. So why should she be punished for being talented but not experienced?

The test was scheduled for first thing Monday and we were still arguing about money on Friday afternoon. Frustrated, I made a few calls and found out that Melinda was a single mom with two young children. I quickly realized she would want this deal finished by end of day so she could get home to her family.

Armed with this personal information, I didn't take any of her calls until after six. At that point, she was furious that I hadn't closed the deal yet.

I told her I was disappointed too but with a little more time, I was sure we could come to an agreement. I explained that I had cancelled my plans for the evening and had just ordered some takeout. If necessary, I was prepared to stay in my office all night to get the deal done.

There was a long pause, then I heard Melinda take a deep breath. She promised to call back in a few minutes. Sure enough, we had a done deal by eight.

And that's all I have to say about that.

Okay, back to Lisa. Her test deal was closed at 30 and 15 which I think is pretty damn good considering she has no real experience. Even if she doesn't book this pilot, I know I'll be able to do better for her next time around.

So now that the paperwork's done, Lisa is ready to test. Five women go to studio and two get cut. Luckily, Lisa is not one of them. That means she moves on to network.

When she's done, Lisa has no idea how she did. The executives didn't laugh but the casting director seemed happy.

At this point, the network has a week to make their decision but in most cases, they have an answer by end of day.

While all this is going on, I sit in my office lighting candles, waiting to hear some news. After what feels like an eternity, the casting director calls with the final word.

It turns out that Lisa got it! She was everyone's favorite from the start and the network is thrilled to have discovered a fresh young talent.

Life is about to become much easier for Lisa. All the casting directors who wouldn't meet her before are now going to be clamoring to bring her in on future projects. Other networks will also be curious about this newcomer who booked a series regular role for the competition.

And by the way, Lisa is not a fictional character. I may have changed her name but the story is 100% true.

The Finish Line

Booking a pilot is great news but it's only the first step. The big question is — will the show get picked up?

By end of April, the pilots have all been completed and presented to the networks. God only knows what really happens behind those closed doors but the fate of every show is usually determined within a few weeks.

During this waiting period, there's a lot of speculation about every pilot's chances. Rumors fly back and forth but the reality is no one knows anything until the official announcements are made in New York.

Right around the second week of May, the networks all gather in the Big Apple for what's known as "The Upfronts". They rent spaces like Carnegie Hall and during the course of several days, everyone announces their new fall schedule.

The network spends a lot of money to fly out every actor who stars in one of the lucky shows that got picked up. These performers are introduced to the advertisers and press with great fanfare.

Now, let's say I booked a series regular on one of these pilots that beat the odds and got picked up by the network. You would think it's finally time to celebrate, right?

Nope.

Here's another one of the many "catches" that are part of pilot season. Just because a show is picked up, it doesn't necessarily mean that all the cast members are going to be picked up with it.

The test deal agreement has an exclusive hold on each series regular until the end of June. That gives the network another month before they have to commit to the entire cast.

During this time, they have the option to recast. Nobody likes doing this but sometimes it's a necessary evil. I've only had it happen a few times but man, I'm always sweating bullets until I get that official pick up notice from the network.

Of course, all this recasting creates a mini pilot season in June which can lead to some very sweet bookings, especially if you've had a lousy pilot season.

Think about it. These shows are no longer pilots; they've all been picked up. So if I book a series regular now, I'm looking at a show that is definitely going to be on the air. And that's major good news.

Pilot season is full of winners and losers at every level. In my career as an agent, I've been at both ends of that equation. But even if I have a really bad year, all I have to do is sit tight for six more months and the whole damn process starts again. And again. And again...

Final Thoughts

Pilot season is the biggest crap shoot in town. The odds of booking a role on a pilot that gets picked up and goes on to become a huge hit like "Friends" are a million to one. Without decent representation, the odds get even worse.

The key to a successful pilot season is to build up your contacts and resume before casting begins. Yes, that can take a long time but in this business, there's no such thing as an overnight success. Remember George Clooney?

Over the years, I've represented plenty of successful actors who have never even tested for a pilot. The truth is not everyone is destined to be a series regular on a hit TV show.

So please don't turn pilot season into the barometer by which you measure your entire career. There's plenty of other work out there to keep you busy for a very long time.

What About Managers?

"People in Hollywood will hem and haw playing all kinds of cute little games, and then you'll finally realize they want something from you. And eventually you'll have to ask, you want something from me, don't you?"

— Steve McQueen

What about Managers?

Sooner or later, every actor takes a long hard look in the mirror and ends up asking themselves the exact same question:

"Do I need a manager?"

It doesn't matter if the actor is established or just getting started. The question always comes up Unfortunately, it's not an easy one to answer.

In my experience, most actors have no idea what a manager does to earn their money. They just know that other actors have one so they want one too.

My feelings about personal managers are extremely mixed. It's a very complicated subject so let's tackle it one step at a time.

So What's A Manager?

Let's make something clear right up front. Managers are not agents.

Talent agents are licensed by the state and follow a strict set of guidelines. Despite recent changes in our relationship with SAG, agents must still maintain a clearly defined office space and can only charge a 10% commission.

Managers, on the other hand, operate without restrictions. There's no governing body that oversees personal managers. They can work out of their homes and they're allowed to charge clients as much as they want.

In other words, *anyone* can be a manager.

How about you? Would you like an exciting career in the world of personal management? No problem. You don't need a license or experience. Hell, you don't even need an office. All you have to do is print up some business cards, sign a few actors and you're good to go.

It's like buying real estate with no money down. Just send me $39.95 and I'll show you how!

As a result, a lot of inexperienced actors are being managed by people lacking the ability and contacts to do their job properly. These actors are trusting their careers to strangers who for the most part, know absolutely nothing about the business of acting.

Now don't get me wrong. There are plenty of first-rate managers out there. The trick is — how do you find them?

The Good, The Bad and The Ugly

Good managers all have a background in the entertainment industry. Many have studio or network experience. Some are even former agents and casting directors looking to expand their horizons.

These managers have well earned connections they can exploit to help their clients. They also have the know-how to advice actors on important career decisions.

In LA, there are many great management/production companies who not only manage talent, they also generate product. This means that they actually help produce films and television shows for some of their more established clients.

If you should be fortunate enough to attract their interest, then you have very little to worry about. These managers are extremely particular about who they sign and usually do their jobs very well.

Then there are the bad managers. I've met several who have absolutely no qualifications to help anyone with their career. They don't really understand the business and usually end up doing more damage than good.

Recently, I met a manager who used to run a dry cleaning business. And that's it. End of resume. The guy liked actors and thought he would give management a shot.

Managers like this, with no industry experience, usually work really hard to find representation for their clients, then sit back and let someone like me do all the work.

So the key to separating the good from the bad is in checking out the person's background. Whenever a new manager calls to introduce themselves, my first question is always "what did you do before becoming a manager?"

This should be your first question too when you're meeting with a manager.

In my opinion, the worst managers are the ones who are former actors. We're talking about people who have failed at their own career and now believe they can do better with someone else. Doesn't that sound promising?

If you end up being managed by an actor who never made it, I would advice you to be careful. There's always a chance that the relationship could turn ugly.

I used to know a pretty young actress named Kate who moved out from New York and signed with a manager named Brenda.

Now, before I go on, there are three things you need to know about this manager:

1) She's in her forties.
2) She wanted to be an actress but never made it.
3) She's not the most attractive woman in the world.

Anyway, Brenda introduced me to Kate and I ended up representing her.

We started setting up auditions and being new to town, Kate would always get very excited about these opportunities. She really wanted to make everyone proud.

And that's when the abuse started.

Without my knowledge, Brenda would tell this poor girl that she wasn't pretty enough to book these parts. She would constantly undermine Kate's confidence by saying she was wasting everyone's time and shouldn't audition for attractive characters.

This went on for months until Kate finally came into my office and told me everything. At this point, she was a total wreck. Her confidence was shot.

It wasn't easy but I got Kate out of her contract with Brenda but it was too little, too late. She ended up moving back home and that's the last I heard of her.

Management Contracts

"You mentioned that Kate had a contract with her manager. Are management contracts different from the ones agents use?"

There are many big differences between the two and that's why you have to be careful when you sign with a manager.

The basic language in an agency contract is dictated by the state and adheres to the law. The agreement is good for 1 year with an option to renew for up to 3 more years.

Management contracts are a little different. Since there are no official restrictions on how they operate, managers are free to generate their own paperwork and can put in any language they want.

For example, managers often ask for long term agreements with no out clause. That means you can't fire your manager. Like it or not, the two of you are a team until the contract expires.

That's why it's a mistake to sign for more than one year. If the manager isn't doing his job, you should have the right to walk away after twelve months.

A lot of management contracts also have automatic renewal clauses. This means that unless you notify your manager in writing that you want to walk away when the contract ends, it automatically rolls over into a brand new contract.

So let's say you signed a three year agreement that's about to expire. You've decided you want to end the relationship but you forget to send written notice. Guess what? You're stuck with the manager for another three long years.

Now let's talk about money. Unlike agents, managers get to commission *all* your earnings as an actor. That includes theatrical, commercial, voice-over, hosting, internet work, residuals, porno, and anything else you can think of.

But it doesn't end there. A lot of managers also take a piece of any and all money you might generate in this business, even if it doesn't involve acting.

So if you write screenplays in your spare time and someone decides to buy one, surprise! Your manager will get a cut of that too.

Managers also have a nasty little habit of writing themselves into all your deals when you start to become successful.

Let's say you're finally breaking out and the studios are lining up to offer you parts. At this point, your manager will start demanding a producing credit and fee for his part in bringing you to the deal.

So on top of commissioning your salary, a manager can also get an additional producing fee for doing a whole lot of nothing.

There have been many stories about inexperienced managers who luck into signing a client who suddenly becomes a star. As a result, they start to make inappropriate demands which ultimately create a lot of negativity around the client. Remember, your manager's behavior will always reflect on you!

If some of these terms sound a little scary, you're free to ask for changes. Remember, everything in life is negotiable and management contracts are no different.

For example, managers used to charge 15% commissions but lately, most of the good ones have cut back to 10. There's really no reason to pay more than that. As an agent, it really freaks me out when I hear that a manager is making more than me for doing less work.

If the idea of negotiating a contract with your new manager makes you uncomfortable, then it's time to get some help. Ask everyone and anyone if they know a lawyer or an agent who might be willing to lend a hand. If that doesn't work, talk to your acting teacher. He might be able to recommend someone.

Naturally, if you already have representation, your agent will be happy to check out the contract and ask for any necessary changes. That's part of our job.

Consider this. When he was young, Bruce Springsteen signed his first management contract on the hood of a parked car. Years later, the Boss found himself in the middle of some pretty expensive litigation so that he could get out of the long term agreement.

So be smart about your future. *Hope for the best but plan for the worst.*

At this point, it occurs to me that I haven't really answered your original question which was, "Do I need a manager?"

Okay, let's try a different approach.

So What Does A Manager Do?

First, let me explain what a manager doesn't do.

By law, a manager is not allowed to solicit work for their clients. This means a manager cannot pitch their clients to casting directors. That's my job.

California's Talent Agency Act requires that anyone who seeks to procure employment for an actor must be a licensed talent agent recognized by the Labor Commission.

So when a manager starts pitching clients and setting up auditions, technically, they're breaking the law. It's called "procurement" and it's 100% illegal.

The law also states that any violation of the act by an unlicensed manager can result in the nullification of any and all contracts and a refund to the performer of any commissions paid to the manager in a one year period before the filing of the complaint.

That's pretty tough talk but let's face it. Actors want as many opportunities as possible and managers know that. So this law gets broken on a regular basis. Except for agents, no one really seems to care.

The bad news for managers is that actors are finally getting hip to this rule and are using it to get out of their contracts. Some actors are even suing their managers for back commissions plus interest. As a result, I predict there are going to be some big changes soon in the way managers do business.

"What else are managers not allowed to do?"

Managers are not allowed to negotiate deals. Again, that's my job. Besides an agent, the only other person allowed to negotiate on behalf of an actor is their lawyer.

If I'm working on a deal for a client who has a manager, the manager is welcome to give me their notes but I'm the only one allowed to talk with the other side. Life is much easier that way.

In the past, I've had managers provide support on complicated deals and by working as a team, we've gotten some really great results.

Unfortunately, I've also been stuck with inexperienced managers who are scared to admit their own ignorance. So instead of asking questions, they panic when a negotiation starts to get hostile.

I remember one manager who lost it in the middle of a very tough deal. The studio wasn't budging on the money and I was threatening to walk away. Luckily, time was on my side. My client had to be on the set in three days so I knew the studio would fold.

I explained this to the manager but she didn't get it. So instead of rolling with it, she called our client and told him the deal was falling apart.

It wasn't. The studio ended up giving me exactly what I wanted. But the poor actor almost had a nervous breakdown.

These are the managers that make me crazy. If she really believed the deal was going bad, then she should've protected her client. Actors are creative people. They don't need to know every little detail. All they care about is the final results.

After the deal was closed, I sent the manager one of my favorite quotes — "Don't speak unless you can improve the silence."

"This is great information but you still haven't answered the question. What exactly does a manager do?"

Yeah, I know. I'm still working on it.

In theory, a personal manager is supposed to take a more hands on approach to an actor's career. Unlike agents, managers only have ten or twelve clients and this gives them enough time to really focus on each individual actor.

Since I have over a hundred clients, there's no way I can give every single one the same amount of attention. It's just not possible.

That's why a lot of actors turn to managers. They want to make sure that someone is thinking about them every single minute of the day.

Good managers usually get involved in all aspects of a client's life — professional and personal. They provide guidance on headshots, training, marketing and if necessary, finding the right agent.

The managers I like are the ones who go the extra mile and try to get their clients meetings with directors who are between projects. This is a great strategy that I don't always have time to do.

I've also seen managers help their clients with personal matters like dating, family problems, buying a home, criminal charges, and even plastic surgery.

Some managers are very tuned in to the Hollywood social scene. They can help get your name on the right guest lists around town. If being seen is important to you, a manager might be helpful.

Other managers are nothing more than hand holders. They take your call every day and commiserate about how difficult it is to be an actor in LA. They're great listeners and that's about it.

Certain actors need someone like this in their life but you have to wonder if it's really worth 10% of all your earnings. Wouldn't a good therapist be cheaper?

Finally, to really comprehend the role of a personal manager, it's important that you understand how the two of us work together.

The Agent/Manager Relationship

As you can imagine, the rise of managers has cluttered the playing field for agents. The good ones leave the pitching to us and only jump in when asked to lend a hand. The bad ones are like a bull in a china shop. They're desperate to make a buck and are constantly getting in the way.

I would say that about a third of my clients have managers. To be honest, some of them work really hard and provide crucial support that makes my job much easier.

For example, one of these managers called recently to remind me that our client had worked with a certain TV director several years ago. I don't always remember little details like that and the information resulted in a major booking.

See? That's a good manager. He did his job really well and didn't cross any lines. Guys like him are worth their weight in gold.

Another manager once provided me with an amazing press kit that helped me sell our client. When I asked where she got it, the manager told me she had put it together in her spare time.

Again, there's another valuable member of the team. This is a manager who knows how to help agents get the job done.

As for the others, I have no idea what they do.

"You're kidding, right?"

No. I really have no idea what they do. Sometimes, weeks go by and I never even speak to them. They just lurk in the shadows until the client books a job. Then they're Johnny on the spot with their opinions.

Other managers read the breakdowns every morning and then waste my time by calling to check if I submitted our client for a role that they're obviously perfect for.

Here's what I mean. Dana is a hot blonde in her twenties who happens to have a manager that I can't stand. Whenever a breakdown comes out for a hot blonde in her twenties, the manager calls to check if I submitted her.

At this point in my life, I've run out of sarcastic answers to that kind of question.

The managers who really alienate agents are the ones who insist on being called first about auditions. They seem to prefer that clients have minimal contact with their agents.

Does that sound like a good idea to you? Wouldn't you rather speak to your agent as much as possible so that you can get to know each other?

When asked why being called first is such a big deal, managers usually respond that it's better if the actor only hears information from one person. That way, there won't be any mistakes.

Excuse me? Am I missing something here? If I'm going to buy into this stupid rule, then shouldn't I be the one to call the client? After all, I'm the one who set up the audition so I have all the details right in front of me. Why go through a middle man?

Obviously, the managers who insist on being called first are suffering from extreme insecurity. They're afraid their client might become too close to the agent and that might lead to someone getting cut from the team.

My strong feelings on this matter can be traced back to the beginning of my career.

When I first became an agent, I made the mistake of always calling my favorite client's manager first with every single audition. I never bothered to call the client directly because I figured what the hell? She already has the information so there's really no reason for us to talk.

You know what happened? The client fired me.

When I called to ask why, the client said all the auditions had been arranged by her manager and as far as she knew, I had done nothing.

For almost an entire year, that damn manager had been taking credit for all my work.

Let me tell you something. It's a good thing there are laws against assault. To this day, I have not worked with that manager again and I never will. His clients are banned for life.

All I can say is — do not allow your manager to create a barrier between you and your agent. That's not in anyone's best interest, especially yours.

"Will my agent hate me if I decide to get a manager?"

No, of course not. Just make sure you speak to your agent first.

Actors often walk into my office and announce they've already signed with a manager. This kind of surprise really upsets me. Agents like to think that our opinion matters and it's very insulting when a client doesn't ask for it.

Besides, how do you know we're going to make a good team? There might be some bad history between us that you're not aware of. Or we may end up having different views on who's going to do what.

Signing with a manager is a big career move and as your agent, I need to be involved in the decision.

And who knows? I might even be open to the idea. If that's the case, I'll probably jump on the phone and set up meetings for you with managers who I believe can help.

If I don't think you need a manager, I'll probably try to change your mind. As long as you listen, I'm not going to get angry if you decide to ignore my advice. Like I said before, it's your career.

So Do I Need A Manager Or Not?

There are two points in an actor's life when a manager can be extremely helpful — the very beginning of your career and when you've finally hit it big.

If you're just starting out, it's hard to find someone who will take a chance on you. Getting an agent isn't easy and casting directors won't meet you unless you have one. That's a major catch 22.

So if you're lucky enough to find a qualified manager who believes in you, I would advice you to sign with him. He'll guide you to the point where you're ready to start working and then he can help you find the right agent.

Despite all my bitching about managers, I have signed some really great actors that I never would have met unless a manager brought them to my attention.

So if you're new to town and things aren't looking so good, the right manager might be able to help you get off to a good start.

A manager can also be useful when you finally hit it big. If your desk is covered with scripts and offers are pouring in, then a good manager will help you make the right choices. They can even help you decide what to wear to the Oscars.

I'm going to assume that the vast majority of actors reading this book aren't worried about the Academy Awards. Most of you are probably trapped in that vague middle ground between getting started and superstardom. You're the ones driving down Sunset Boulevard, dazed and confused, wondering if you need a manager.

My answer is — I don't know.

Honestly, I really don't. There are so many factors at work that it's almost impossible for me to give you an honest answer. So much of it depends on the individual person and their needs.

Hopefully, this chapter has provided you with enough information to make the right decision.

In closing, here's a list of questions you need to ask before you sign with a manager:

1) What's your background?
2) How many clients do you have?
3) Who are those clients?
4) Are they working?
5) Do they all have agents?
6) Which talent agencies do you work with?
7) Do you have a lot of friends in casting?
8) What exactly can I expect from you?
9)
10)

I left the last two blank for you to fill in. Give it some serious thought, then add a couple of questions that directly address your own personal needs.

Final Thoughts

Think of yourself as a professional quarterback. It doesn't matter if you're talented. You still need to surround yourself with a great team or you're going to get creamed.

When agents and managers put aside their egos and focus on a client's career, wonderful things can happen. Their united strength can open a lot of closed doors and help create some amazing opportunities.

There's no doubt about it. The right manager at the right time can make a big difference in your life. There are some really great ones out there who genuinely care about actors and want to see their clients succeed.

But like I said before, it's easy to get stuck with a lemon. The wrong manager can do more harm than good. I've seen a lot of talented actors fail because of bad management.

So be smart about who you invite to join your team. Use the information in this chapter to empower yourself with knowledge. And if you have any doubts about the person you're dealing with, run for the hills!

Rules of the Game

"All you need are fifty good breaks..."

— Walter Matthau

Rules of the Game 9

The sad truth is that most people who decide to pursue a career in acting have no idea how stacked the deck is against them.

Success is often based on luck and timing, not skill and ability. It's one of the few jobs out there where talent will not always lead to work.

Here's how the Bureau of Labor Statistics describes the profession of acting:

"Acting demands patience and total commitment, because there are often long periods of unemployment between jobs. While under contract, actors are frequently required to work long hours and travel. For stage actors, flawless performances require tedious memorizing of lines and repetitive rehearsals, and in television, actors must deliver good performances with very little preparation. Actors need stamina to withstand hours under hot lights, heavy costumes and make-up, physically demanding tasks, long, irregular schedules, and the adverse weather and living conditions that may exist on location shoots. And actors face the constant anxiety of intermittent employment and regular rejection when auditioning for work."

The guy who wrote this is right on target. The life of an actor is extremely difficult. You have to deal with constant rejection. You're always struggling to make ends meet. And you end up spending more time looking for work than actually working.

The way I see it, you have to be a little bit crazy to actually choose acting as your career.

So now that we're nearing the end of this book, I'm going to leave you with ten simple rules that might help you survive this insane business. Following these rules will not guarantee you success but they should make your life a lot easier.

And hopefully, a lot happier.

 **Learn Your Craft**

The majority of actors who fail in this business are simply not good enough. That's why you should always be striving to become a better actor. True talent can never be denied.

Real actors are always in class, studying hard and working on their craft. You can also find them on stage, honing their skills and learning how to reach a live audience.

Remember, acting is about technique and the more you work on yours, the greater chance you'll have to succeed.

 **Know the Business**

Being an artist isn't enough. If you want to survive, you have to learn the business side of acting too.

So empower yourself with as much knowledge as possible. Study what's happening in the industry. A smart actor will always go further than an ignorant one.

 **Make Alliances**

This is what it takes to win on "Survivor" and this is what it takes to succeed in life. You just can't do it alone.

Seek out others who can help you accomplish your goals. Find mentors to guide you on the path to success. Make them part of your team.

You should also share your knowledge with the other actors in your life. Include them in your plans. If you lend a hand, they might do the same for you.

4 Don't Forget about Money

This is a big one. You need to make a living while you're chasing your dream. If you're constantly worried about paying the rent, you won't be able to focus on your goals.

So find a job (or two) that will generate income and give you enough freedom to go out on auditions. Money isn't everything but it sure helps in this town.

5 Work Hard

Having a great work ethic is very important. Think about it. The average person spends about 40 hours a week working at their job. If you're not spending at least that much time on your career, then sorry, acting is just a hobby.

You should always be studying, doing workshops, going to plays, and everything else possible to advance your career. Lazy actors don't last long in this business.

 **Set Demanding Goals**

Working hard isn't good enough. You need to have a purpose, a sense of direction.

Challenge yourself by setting artistic and professional goals in all areas of your life. Start off with short-term goals that are easy to reach, then make the goals more demanding as you begin to achieve success.

Doing this will not only help your career, it will also give you a great feeling of accomplishment.

 **Take Chances**

You should do something every day that scares you. Playing it safe gets you nowhere fast.

Try making choices in acting class that are way outside your safety zone. Or consider approaching someone in the industry who doesn't know you and probably doesn't want to know you. What's the worst that can happen?

Remember, success is often born on a chance.

 **Be Realistic**

Actors are dreamers who sometimes get lost in a world of make believe. That's why it's important to be honest with yourself about your level of talent and how much progress you're making in this business. There is nothing sadder than a life wasted in the pursuit of a goal that can never be reached.

So set a time limit of 5 years to discover if you should really be pursuing a career in acting. In that time, you need to have solid evidence that you're doing the right thing. That evidence can be in the form of repeated employment or genuine praise from many different sources in the business.

 **Live Your Life**

It saddens me when actors say they're putting life on hold while they pursue their career. You have to remember that acting is based on life experience. So how can you be a great actor if you have no life?

Do yourself a favor and take a day off every now and then. Go hiking in the canyons. Or take a drive up the coast. Whatever. Just don't forget to live!

 Act!

This business can break your heart. I've seen it happen a million times. But you should never allow anything to destroy your love of acting.

So my advice is get out there and act! I don't care if it's in a play or a student film. Just find those creative moments that give you pleasure. They will keep your dreams alive while you're waiting for the phone to ring.

"If you want to be an actor, act. It's really simple. The more you act, the better you get. Go to classes. Go to workshops. Act more hours of the day than not. Act for free. And if you're lucky, every once in a while, you'll get paid."

— Richard Dreyfuss

ACKNOWLEDGEMENTS

First, I have to thank my good friend from down under, Jeff Bollow. Without his help and support, this book never would've been published. He paved the way and warned me about the traps that were hidden along the path. Thanks, mate.

I also have to express my gratitude to Anne Flanagan for her sharp eye and critical mind. Besides being an excellent writer in her own right, Anne has always been there when I need an honest voice.

I should also acknowledge Susan Calogerakis for giving me my very first job in the agency business. To this day, I still organize my desk exactly like hers. *(For the record, I always wondered if the only reason Susan hired me to be her assistant was because I could pronounce her last name.)*

Over the years, I've had the privilege of working with some really great agents like Frank Balkin, Geneva Bray, Larry Corsa, Tom Harrison, J. Morgan, Gwenn Pepper, Adrienne Spitzer and Kevin "Truck" Turner. Their friendship and support have made a tough job much easier.

I also have to thank all the exhausted assistants out there who have worked so hard to make me look good. I'd especially like to mention Alex Stewart who is without a doubt, the hardest working man in show business.

And finally, I have to express my gratitude to Craig Wyckoff. Craig took a chance when he made me an agent and his faith in my ability has made all the difference in my career.

Thanks, big guy.

RECOMMENDED READING

Like I said at the beginning, there are some really lousy books out there about the business of acting. Here are some of the good ones:

THE LA AGENT BOOK & HOW TO SELL YOURSELF AS AN ACTOR by K. Callan. These popular books are packed with extremely valuable information and they're updated on a regular basis. No actor should be without them.

NEXT! AN ACTORS GUIDE TO AUDITIONING by Ellie Kanner. Ellie is a former casting director who really knows her stuff.

HOW TO GET THE PART...WITHOUT FALLING APART by Margie Haber. Written by one of LA's top acting teachers, this book is considered must reading for all actors.

ACTOR'S ENCLOPEDIA OF CASTING DIRECTORS by Karen Kondazian. This is a collection of candid interviews with almost every casting director in the business.

HOW TO AGENT YOUR AGENT by Nancy Rainford. Another title for this great book would be "Everything You Always Wanted To Know About Your Agent But Were Afraid To Ask".

HOLLYWOOD RAT RACE by Ed Wood Jr. A hysterical collection of advice for actors from the director of "Plan 9 From Outer Space" — the worst movie ever made.

For more information or
additional copies, log on to
www.AnAgentTellsAll.com.

Professional organizations will
also find information about
booking Tony Martinez for
personal appearances and
motivational seminars.